siberian husky

understanding and
caring for your breed

Written by
Robert Lockwood

siberian husky

understanding and
caring for your breed

Written by **Robert Lockwood**

Pet Book Publishing Company

The Old Hen House, St Martin's Farm, Zeals, Warminster, Wiltshire,
BA12 6NZ, United Kingdom.

Printed by Printworks Global Ltd., London & Hong Kong

ISBN: 978-1-910488-30-0

Contents

Introducing the Siberian Husky

The stunning Siberian Husky, who looks more like a wolf than a dog, is now the breed of choice for a worldwide band of enthusiasts. So what is it that draws people to this enigmatic dog from the far North?

The Siberian Husky was bred to pull light loads over long distances, in the harshest of conditions, and he is built for the job. Every aspect of his conformation reflects the gruelling demands imposed upon him and, as such, he is a masterpiece in canine physiology.

He is a medium-sized dog who is quick and light on his feet. Although he is strong and muscular, he moves with freedom and grace. For the Siberian

Husky the name of the game is speed and endurance rather than pure power, and so he has the construction of a top-class athlete.

He has a deep chest which allows plenty of space for heart and lungs, his shoulders are well laid back and his back is strong and straight. His job was to pull a light load – two or three times his own bodyweight – which means that power must come from the hindquarters, propelling him forwards, with the forequarters taking most of the impact.

Working in sub-zero temperatures, the Siberian Husky needed a coat to protect him – and all Sibe owners will testify to the fact that the has a coat and a half!

The top coat is medium in length and the guard hairs give some protection, but it is the dense undercoat that gives the real insulation. This is shed twice a year – and the amount of hair that will fill your house is truly amazing.

The Siberian can be any colour and he often has striking markings on his head that are not seen in other breeds. His head is in proportion to his body, with a medium length muzzle.

The triangular-shaped ears are pricked and alert, and the almond-shaped eyes are set obliquely, giving a slightly oriental look. The eyes can be blue, brown, or one of each colour, and the typical expression is one of keenness – maybe with a hint of mischievousness...

Living with a Siberian Husky

There was a time when the Siberian Husky was little known outside his native home of northern Siberia. Bred to work in a team, pulling loads across ice and snow, he does not appear to have the makings of a pet. However he has proved doubters wrong and, in the right hands, he is a superb companion dog.

This is a specialist breed and it is vitally important to look beyond his appearance. Unfortunately, too many people are attracted by his striking good looks and rush out to buy a Siberian without weighing up the pros and cons.

On the plus side, the Siberian Husky is friendly and out-going and will bond closely with his human family. He gets on well with children, as long as ground rules are observed on both sides. He is a naturally clean dog and will settle in any household – big or small, town or country.

However, the Siberian Husky has the mindset of a hunting dog and, given the opportunity, he will pursue any small, furry animal, and will be deaf to your calls. This means that he cannot be trusted off-lead unless you have access to a safe, enclosed exercise area. This has obvious drawbacks with regard to caring for him and integrating him in family life.

The ideal Siberian owner needs to be as keen on exercise as his dog! If a Sibe cannot be given free running exercise, it is up to the owner to provide a substitute. Ideally, this will mean taking part in a sport such as canicross, mushing or bikejoring (see page 152) which will give him the perfect outlet for his considerable energy.

It is also important to bear in mind that a dog with a high drive and a strong prey instinct will regard all small animals as fair game, and that includes the family cat, rabbit or guinea pig. With hard work and training, a Siberian can learn to live with a cat but, again, he can never be entirely trusted.

He may come to understand that the family cat is off limits, but he will not show the same restraint with your neighbours' cats, which could cause major problems.

On the plus side, the Siberian Husky was bred to work in a team, and he is generally friendly and sociable with other dogs.

The Siberian is a highly intelligent working dog and he needs to use his brain. If he is bored or frustrated he will quickly make up is own agenda – and you will not be impressed. A Siberian will resort to barking, howling, and destructive behaviour – and he will make your life a misery. However, with the mental stimulation that comes from training and taking part in an organised activity, a Siberian will realise his potential as a first-rate companion dog.

Below: This is a breed that needs physical exercise and mental stimulation.

Tracing back in time

The Siberian Husky has a history that stretches back thousands of years when the Chukchi people of Northern Siberia developed a dog that could be both helpmate and companion. DNA tests have revealed that the Sibe is one of the oldest of all known dog breeds.

In the frozen wastes of Siberia the Chukchi travelled from their settlements in the Kolyma River basin to the coast to hunt seals. Once they had a reasonable haul, they needed to transport their catch home. This was no easy matter as long distances had to be covered in sub-zero temperatures. The Chuckchi needed to find a way of transporting their precious cargo quickly and efficiently.

The solution was to develop teams of dogs that could pull sleds over long distances. It was important to keep up a moderate speed but the dogs also

needed to keep going for long periods. When there was the opportunity to rest, food was scarce so the dogs needed to survive on modest rations, sleeping outside in the harshest of conditions.

The dogs had to work and live together in close proximity, so they had to get on with each other. A sound temperament was therefore of paramount importance. In terms of working ability, they needed to take orders but lead dogs also needed to show initiative, sometimes ignoring instructions if the terrain was unsafe.

Quite a tall order, but over successive generations, the Chukchi developed a husky that was perfect for the job. These dogs were so highly valued that they became more than working dogs. They were invited into the homes of the Chukchi and became loyal and loving family companions.

Changing times

The Chukchi way of life continued undisturbed for many centuries and the Siberian Husky was unknown outside his native home. But when gold was discovered in Alaska in the late 19th century, there was a sudden and urgent need for dogs who could pull sleds. In the desperate rush to get to the gold, money was no object and sled dogs changed hands for exorbitant sums.

It is not known exactly when the first Siberian Huskies arrived in Alaska, but the first documentary evidence is dated 1909 when a team of Sibes competed in a long distance sled race called the All Alaska Sweepstakes. A Russian fur trader, named William Goosak imported his team from Siberia. His dogs were much lighter in build than the other sled dog teams that were entered, and his dogs were labelled the 'Siberian rats'.

Starting at odds of 100-1, they surprised everyone when they finished third, only beaten out of first place because they were not rested properly during the course of the race. Nevertheless, the Siberian Husky earned a reputation for his speed and endurance, and was soon highly sought after in sled dog teams.

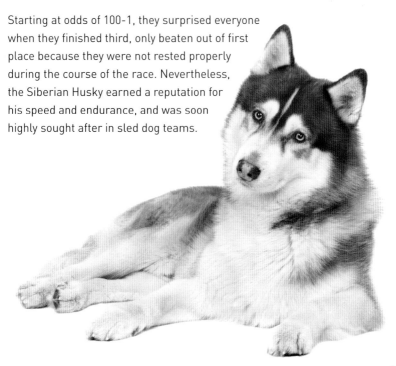

Below: Selective breeding has produced a loyal companion dog with a first class work ethic.

Developing the breed

The Siberian Husky was gradually gaining wider recognition but following the events of 1925, the breed went international.

In that year, there was an outbreak of diptheria in Nome, Alaska, and the local doctor reported that his supply of serum was running out. Serum could be provided by a hospital in Anchorage but the question was how to get it there in the depths of winter in sub zero temperatures and with winds of 80 miles an hour?

It was decided to transport the serum by train as far as Nenana, leaving a journey of 674 miles to Nome. The only possible transport was by dog sled, and it was estimated that the journey would take a dog sled team a minimum of 25 days.

To cut down on time, a relay system was devised, with fresh dogs and drivers waiting at roundhouses along the route.

Heroic feats were performed by a number of dog sled teams, including Leonhard Seppala's team, led by 12-year-old Togo, who completed the longest leg – 84 miles in one day – in the worst conditions.

The final section was completed by Gunnar Kaasen and his team, and the serum reached Nome in an incredible five and a half days.

During the relay, newspapers all over the United States published daily bulletins, and at its successful conclusion the dogs and their drivers were stars. Both Kaasen and Seppala toured the US with their dogs, and a film, Balto's Race to Nome, featured Kaasen's lead dog.

An adopted breed

Leonhard Seppala's contribution to the breed's recognition did not stop at the serum run. He settled in the USA and went into partnership with Elizabeth Ricker at her Poland Spring kennels.

They bred from Seppala's existing dogs and also imported new bloodlines from Siberia. This eventually became impossible under Communist rule, but Sappala had done enough to get the Siberian Husky established in a new home.

A number of kennels were instrumental in developing the breed in the early days, drawing up a

Breed Standard, and breeding dogs that could work and meet the stipulations of the show ring.

Always a specialist breed, the first Siberian Huskies did not reach the UK until 1968. A breed club was set up in 1977 and the breed finally achieved Championship status in 1986.

The current scene

The Siberian Husky reached its height of popularity in the United States in the 1980s, and has since declined with entries at shows sometimes in single numbers. Sibes are used for racing, but, at the present time, the Alaskan Malamute is favoured.

In contrast, the Siberian Husky has taken the UK by storm in its short history. Dry land racing has a big following, show entries are rising, and the Siberian is also a highly valued companion dog. However popularity comes at a price, and the number of Siberians being bred by unscrupulous money-makers is growing.

Devotees of the breed are working hard to ensure that only the best dogs are bred from, and that Siberian puppies only go to dedicated owners who can truly care for this extraordinary breed.

What should a Siberian Husky look like?

This sled dog from the North is built for power, speed and endurance. There is no hint of exaggeration in his athletic body and yet his graceful outline, his amazing fur coat, and his distinctive facial expression, make him one of the most admired of breeds. What makes a Siberian so special?

If you speak to most owners of Siberians they will tell you they have the perfect dog and, of course, they do. Pet owners are not looking for perfection as in the showing world; they are looking for the dog that is perfect for what they want. As long as he is obedient, has a good temperament and is easy to live with, he is perfect in their eyes.

In the world of show dogs, the perfect dog does not and will never exist; every dog has his faults. All breeders can do is strive to produce a dog that is fit for function and adheres as closely as possible to the Breed Standard, which is the written blueprint describing what the breed should look like. In the show ring, the judge does not compare dog against dog, but each dog against the Breed Standard. The dog that, in their opinion, comes nearest to the Standard, is the winner. However the Breed Standard is open to interpretation and because of this you don't get the same dog winning all the time.

There are a number of governing bodies that authorise Breed Standards, most notably the Kennel Club in the UK, the American Kennel Club and the Federation Cynologique Internationale (FCI) which legislates for 89 member countries. There are minor differences between the Standards, but all agree on the essentials which means all three varieties can be shown successfully worldwide.

General Appearance

The Siberian Husky is a medium-sized sled dog who is quick and light on his feet. He should never be mistaken for the heavier freight animals such as the Alaskan Malamute.

His compact, well-balanced body, his heavy coat, erect ears and furred tail reflect his northern heritage. Males are masculine looking but never coarse; females are feminine but there should be no weakness of structure.

Temperament

The Siberian is a friendly, gentle dog and a most willing worker. He should show no trace of suspicion with strangers or aggression with other dogs, but a measure of reserve and dignity is expected in the mature dog. He is intelligent and although he is tractable, he also has an independent streak.

Head and skull

Everything about the Siberian Husky is balanced and in proportion and so his medium-sized head is directly in proportion with his body. The skull is slightly rounded on top and tapers from the widest point to the eyes. It is finely chiselled giving a fox-like appearance.

The muzzle is medium in length and tapers gradually to a rounded nose. The stop – the step-up between the muzzle and the forehead – is clearly defined. The colour of the nose complements the coat colour:

Black in grey, tan or black dogs

Liver in copper dogs

Flesh-coloured in white dogs

In the winter, the nose may be pink-streaked, which is known as a 'snow nose'.

Eyes

The Siberian Husky has the most compelling eyes. They are medium-sized and almond shaped; they are set obliquely which means they have an upwards tilt at the corners.

This trait is in common with other Northern breeds as forward facing or prominent eyes would be more susceptible to injury from driving snow and ice.

The colour of the eyes is another feature of the breed; they can be any shade of blue or brown, one of each colour or parti-coloured. The typical Siberian expression is keen and interested.

Ears

Again moderation is key; the ears are medium-sized in proportion with the head. They are triangular in shape, and set high on the head.

They are strongly erect, slightly arched at the back, with rounded tips. To withstand the extreme cold, the ears are well-furred both inside and out.

Points of anatomy

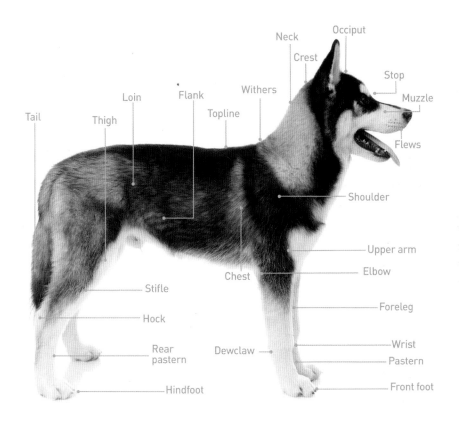

Neck

Occiput

Crest

Stop

Muzzle

Withers

Flews

Loin

Flank

Topline

Tail

Thigh

Shoulder

Upper arm

Elbow

Chest

Stifle

Foreleg

Hock

Wrist

Rear
pastern

Dewclaw

Pastern

Hindfoot

Front foot

Mouth

The lips are tight fitting and well pigmented. The jaws are strong with a perfect scissor bite, which means the teeth on the upper jaw closely overlap the teeth on the lower jaw.

Neck

The neck is medium in both length and thickness. When a Siberian is standing, it is carried proudly erect; when he is on the move the neck is extended so the head is carried slightly forward.

Forequarters

The shoulder blades are well laid back and the muscle holding the chest to the ribcage is firm and well developed.

Viewed from the front, the forelegs are moderately spaced, parallel and straight with elbows close to the body.

Body

The back is straight and strong with a level topline from the withers (the highest point of the shoulder) to the croup (the area between the pin bones and the tail). It is of medium length with taut loins which are narrower than the ribcage.

The chest is deep and strong, with plenty of lung-room for this endurance breed. It should not be too broad and the deepest point should be level with the elbows.

Hindquarters

Viewed from the rear, the hind legs are moderately spaced and parallel. The upper thighs are well muscled; the stifles (knee joints) are well bent and the hocks (ankle joints) are set low to the ground.

It is the hindquarters that propel the Siberian forwards, and for a sled dog pulling a load, they need to be strong, muscular and powerful.

Feet

The feet are compact and oval in shape, specifically designed for running in snow. The pads are tough and thickly cushioned; fur grows between the toes and pads.

Tail

The fox-like brush tail is well-furred and is set below the level of the topline. When a Siberian is at attention, the tail is carried in a graceful curve over the back. In repose or when working, a trailing tail is normal.

Movement

The Siberian Husky's gait (movement) should appear smooth and totally effortless. He is quick and light on his feet, showing good reach from the front and good drive from the rear when he is trotting. This is the pace that is required in the show ring, but a working Siberian will lope or gallop.

Coat

The Siberian Husky was bred to work in extreme temperatures and so a protective, insulating coat is vital. The double coat consists of an outer coat of smooth, straight guard hairs, and a soft, dense undercoat.

The outer coat is medium in length which allows the dog to look well-furred, but also to maintain his clean-cut outline. A long, rough or shaggy coat is penalised in the show ring, as is a texture that is too harsh or too silky.

Colour

The Siberian comes in a wonderful array of colours – any colour from black to pure white is allowed and no colour is favoured.

Markings on the head are common, and these include a variety of striking patterns.

Size

The ideal size for a Siberian Husky is assessed in terms of both size and weight. The permitted height for males is 53-60cm (21-23.5in), females should be between 51-56cm (20-22in). Weight should be in proportion to height with males weighing 20-27kg (45-60lb), and females 16-23kg (35-50lb).

Summing up

The majority of Siberian Huskies are kept as pets and as competition dogs and will never be exhibited in the show ring.

However, it is important that breeders strive for perfection and try to produce dogs that adhere as closely as possible to the Breed Standard. The top priority is to breed dogs that are both typical of the breed and sound in mind and body.

Coat colour and markings are a distinctive feature of the breed.

What do you want from your Sibe?

There are hundreds of pedigree dog breeds to choose from so how can you be sure that the Siberian Husky is the right dog for you? The Sibe can be challenging to own so you need to be 100 per cent confident that this is the breed that is best suited to your lifestyle.

Companion

The Siberian is a loving and loyal dog and will show great affection for all members of his human family. He gets on well with children as long as a sense of mutual respect is established.

He will generally thrive in a home where there are

older children as there will be more opportunities for providing an active lifestyle.

If you are frail or getting on in years, a Siberian is not the breed for you. This is a dog that needs strenuous exercise and if this is not provided he will become bored and resort to deviant behaviour such as being destructive or barking continually.

The problem is exacerbated because you cannot give a Siberian free running exercise unless you are in a fenced area. His hunting drive is so strong that he will pick up on the first scent he comes across – and he will be off!

Even if you have trained a good response to the recall at home (see page 134), a Sibe cannot be trusted in new, exciting environments.

Tragically, all too many Siberian Huskies have been killed in road traffic accidents because their desire to run and hunt has overtaken all other considerations.

The Siberian is an intelligent dog and can be trained to a good level of domestic obedience. However, this is a tough, strong-willed dog who is ready to take the initiative.

Training needs to be motivational and rewarding; the Siberian will be easily bored by repetition.

If you are looking for a guard dog, you will be

disappointed. The Siberian loves people and will welcome everyone into his home with boundless enthusiasm!

Sports dog

The Siberian Husky was bred to pull sleds at moderate speed over great distances – and this is where his true talents lie.

This job may be redundant in the modern world, but it has been adapted to the sports arena and mushing is now a highly competitive and highly addictive discipline which can take place over dry land as well as over snow and ice.

The Siberian Husky is the perfect choice if you want to get involved in one of the more energetic canine sports.

There are other sports, such as canicross, which are tailor-made for Siberians as it is an effective way of providing exercise and mental stimulation. Sibes are also successful in agility and off-shoots of mushing which include scootering and skijoring.

However, if your interest lies in competitive obedience, a Siberian is not the obvious candidate. He is highly intelligent, but will quickly lose interest if he does not see a point to what he is doing.

For more information, see Opportunities for Siberians, page 148.

Show dog

The Siberian Husky looks spectacular in the show ring, and it is one of the few breeds that has not been adapted to meet the demands of the show world; a show Siberian is still fully capable of carrying out the job he was bred to do.

In terms of presentation, the Siberian is straightforward, as any attempt to trim the coat to enhance his appearance is frowned upon. If you plan to exhibit your Siberian, you will need to work hard at his training and socialisation so that he can cope with the pressures of the show ring.

For more information on showing, see page 155.

Facing page: Showing is a specialist hobby which can become highly addictive!

What
does your
Siberian
want from
you?

A dog cannot speak for himself, so we need to view the world from a canine perspective and work out what a Siberian Husky needs in order to live a happy, contented and fulfilling life.

Time and commitment

First of all, a Siberian Husky needs a commitment that you will care for him for the duration of his life – guiding him through his puppyhood, enjoying his adulthood, and being there for him in his later years.

If all potential owners were prepared to make this pledge, there would be scarcely any dogs in rescue.

The Siberian has a high prey drive and needs extensive exercise. He is an intelligent dog who is easily bored. This is a challenging combination which means that Sibe owners must be dedicated to providing a lifestyle that suits this amazing breed.

As already highlighted, free running exercise is not often a safe option and so time and effort is required to provide other options.

Taking part in one of the canine sports where the Sibe excels, such as mushing or canicross, is the ideal solution, but you will need to train your dog and then give up time to participate. For a dedicated, obsessed owner, this is no hardship – but it is not for the faint-hearted.

If you take on a Siberian thinking he will be content as a family pet, taking limited on-lead exercise, with no outlet for his mental energy, you will end up with a problem dog. A bored, frustrated Siberian will make his feelings very evident by becoming destructive, demanding and often unbearably vocal, which will not go down well with the neighbours.

If you cannot give your Siberian the time and commitment he needs, this is not the breed for you. In addition, if you have to go out to work and leave your dog for more than four hours, you should delay owning a dog of any breed until your circumstances change.

Practical matters

If you are a house-proud, do not get a Siberian Husky! In order to withstand sub-zero temperatures, the Siberian needed major insulation which comes in the form of a double coat.

Twice a year, the coat will shed, and you will be flabbergasted by the hair that comes out. This process lasts for several weeks, and no amount of vacuuming can keep pace with the hair that covers carpets, furniture and clothes. Again, this is part and parcel of owning a Siberian, but it is definitely something you and your family should consider before taking on this very special breed.

For information on coat care, see page 106.

Training and leadership

The Siberian Husky is a clever dog but he does not come ready-trained – far from it! This is a dog that was bred to work closely with people, but he also needed to be a decision-maker. If his musher commanded him to pull a sled over thin ice for example, he had to take the initiative and by-pass the request.

This requires intelligence and strength of character, which are virtues in a working dog but need to be channelled in a domestic setting. A Siberian needs to understand his place in the family circle and to respect your role as provider and decision-maker.

This does not mean that you need to adopt bullying tactics; the key is firm, fair and consistent training so your Sibe always knows his boundaries.

If you work at this from the moment your Siberian comes to live with you, you will be rewarded with a thinking dog that is prepared to listen to you.

Facing page: An active life should be considered essential for the Siberian Husky.

Extra considerations

Now you have decided that a Siberian Husky is the dog of your dreams, you can narrow your choice so you know exactly what you are looking for.

Male or female?

Whether you get a male or female Siberian Husky comes down to personal preference. The male is bigger and stronger, so this may be a consideration depending on your own physical capabilities. Generally, the female Siberian is considered to be a little more aloof than the male and she has more of an independent spirit. The male is often found to be more affectionate than the female and less hormonal.

If you decide on a female, you will need to cope with her seasons, which will start at around nine months and will occur twice-yearly thereafter. During the three-week period of a season, you will need to

keep your bitch away from entire males (males that have not been neutered) to eliminate the risk of an unwanted pregnancy. Some owners report that females may be a little moody and withdrawn during their seasonal cycle and if they suffer phantom pregnancy symptoms post-season, they may be protective of resources, such as food and beds. If you have more than one female dog, you may find that trouble can occur when one is in season.

Many pet owners opt for neutering, which puts an end to the seasons, and also has many attendant health benefits. The operation, known as spaying, is usually carried out at some point after the first season. The best plan is to seek advice from your vet.

An entire male may not cause many problems, although some do have a stronger tendency to mark, which could include in the house. However, training will usually put a stop to this. An entire male will also be on the lookout for bitches in season, and this may lead to difficulties, depending on your circumstances.

Neutering (castrating) a male is a relatively simple operation, and there are associated health benefits. It may inhibit overly 'male' behaviour, but it should not be seen as a cure for established behavioural problems. If behaviour has become ingrained, castration is unlikely to make a difference. The timing of surgery is also significant; the best plan is seek advice from your vet.

More than one?

Siberian Huskies were bred to work in teams and there is no doubt they enjoy canine company. For those who get seriously involved in mushing, a multi-dog household becomes inevitable.

But regardless of whether you plan to keep two Siberians, or a pack, you need to allow a decent gap between acquiring new additions. Do not make the mistake of getting two pups from the same litter, or even two youngsters who are close in age. The pups will have a great time, but they will bond with each other rather than with you. House training will be a nightmare, and unless you are truly dedicated and are prepared to allocate individual time for each dog, training will be a disaster.

If you take on a second Siberian, wait at least 18 months so your first dog is fully trained and settled before embarking on a puppy. Same sex pairs and mixed pairs seem to get on equally well but if you opt for a male and a female you will need to get one or both neutered. If you are running a pack of Siberians, mixing sexes becomes highly complicated.

You either need a huge amount of space to keep the sexes separated during seasons, or make a decision to neuter one gender.

An older dog

You may decide to miss out on the puppy phase and take on an older dog instead. Such a dog may be harder to track down, but sometimes a breeder will rehome a female when her breeding career is at an end so she will enjoy the benefits of getting more individual attention. The breeder may run on a puppy as a show prospect, but if that potential is not realised the dog may be better suited to a pet home.

There are advantages to taking on an older dog, as you know exactly what you are getting. But the upheaval of changing homes can be quite upsetting, so you will need to have plenty of patience during the settling in period.

Rehoming a rescued dog

The Siberian Husky is becoming increasingly popular – and this is not always to his advantage. People are attracted by the breed's stunning good looks but do not always consider the implications of owning an independent-minded, high-drive dog who needs extensive but controlled exercise. Inevitably there are mismatches which means dogs end up in rescue. You

Facing page: An older dog may be the best option for you and your family.

may find a Siberian Husky in an all breed rescue shelter, but breed clubs run their own rescue schemes, and this may be a better option.

A dog may find himself in rescue through no fault of his own, mostly when a family's circumstances change. The reasons are various, ranging from illness or death of the original owner to family breakdown, changing jobs, or even the arrival of a new baby.

However, in the case of a Siberian, it could be because he was in the 'wrong' home and his family failed to cope with his needs. If you decide you want to take on a rescued dog, you need to be very sure that you can cope with the demands of this breed. In addition, there may be behavioural issues resulting from a poor upbringing which you may need to resolve.

The first step is to find out as much as you can about the dog's history so you know exactly what you are taking on. You need to be aware of his age and health status, his likes and dislikes, plus any behavioural problems that may be relevant.

You need to be realistic about what you are capable of achieving so you can be sure you can give the dog in question a permanent home. Regardless of the dog's previous history, you will need to give him plenty of time and be patient with him as he settles into his new home. It may take weeks, or even months before he becomes fully integrated in the family, but if all goes well you will have the reward of knowing that you have given a Siberian a second chance.

Below: Could you give a rescued dog a second chance?

Sourcing a puppy

Your aim is to find a healthy Siberian puppy that has been reared with the greatest possible care. Where do you start?

A tried-and-trusted method of finding a puppy is to attend a dog show where your chosen breed is being exhibited. The classes are divided between males and females and are age related so you will see puppies from as young as six months, veterans, and everything in between.

You will be able to see a wide range of colours and markings and, if you look closely, you will also see there are differences in 'type'.

They are all purebred Siberian Huskies but breeders produce dogs with a family likeness, so you can see which type you prefer.

When judging has been completed, talk to the exhibitors and find out more about their dogs. They may not have puppies available, but some will be planning a litter, and you may decide to put your name on a waiting list.

Internet research

The Internet is an excellent resource, but when it comes to finding a puppy, use it with care:

DO go to the website of your national Kennel Club.

Both the American Kennel Club (AKC) and the Kennel Club (KC) have excellent websites which will give you information about the Siberian Husky as a breed, and what to look for when choosing a puppy. You will also find contact details for specialist breed clubs (see below).

Both sites have lists of puppies available, and you can look out for breeders of merit (AKC) and assured breeders (KC) which indicates that a code of conduct has been adhered to.

DO find details of specialist breed clubs.

On breed club websites you will find lots of useful information which will help you to care for your Siberian. There may be contact details of breeders in your area, or you may need to go through the club secretary. Some websites also have a list of breeders that have puppies available. The advantage of going through a breed club is that members will follow a code of ethics, and this will give you some guarantees regarding breeding stock and health checks.

If you are planning to exhibit your Siberian Husky you will want to find a breeder that has had some success in the show ring. Show lines and working lines are not divided, as they are in many breeds,. However if you plan to work your Siberian, it worth attending rallies and talking to winning teams so you can discover which bloodlines are being used and if there are litters becoming available.

DO NOT look at puppies for sale.

There are legitimate Siberian Husky breeders with their own websites, and they may, occasionally, advertise a litter, although in most cases reputable breeders have waiting lists for their puppies.

The danger comes from unscrupulous breeders that produce puppies purely for profit, with no thought for the health of the dogs they breed from and no care given to rearing the litter.

Colours are advertised as being 'rare' and offered at a higher price, but this is a nonsense. In Siberian Huskies all colours and markings are of equal value.

Photos of puppies are hard to resist, but never make a decision based purely on an advertisement. You need to find out who the breeder is, and have the opportunity to visit their premises and inspect the litter before making a decision.

Questions, questions, questions

When you find a breeder with puppies available, you will have lots of questions to ask. These should include the following:

- Where have the puppies been reared? Hopefully, they will be in a home environment which gives them the best possible start in life.

- How many are in the litter?

- What is the split of males and females?

- What colours are available?

- How many have already been spoken for? The breeder will probably be keeping a puppy to show or for breeding, and there may be others on a waiting list.

- Can I see the mother with her puppies?

- What age are the puppies?

- When will they be ready to go to their new homes?

Bear in mind puppies need to be with their mother and siblings until they are a minimum of eight weeks of age otherwise they miss out on vital learning and communication skills which will have a detrimental effect on them for the rest of their lives.

You should also be prepared to answer a number of searching questions so the breeder can check if you are suitable as a potential owner of one of their precious puppies.

You will be asked some or all of the following questions:

Below: Find out how the puppies have been reared.

- What is your home set up?

- Do you have children/grandchildren?

- What are their ages?

- Is there somebody at home the majority of the time?

- What is your previous experience with dogs?

- Do you already have other dogs at home?

- Do you want to exhibit your Siberian Husky in the show ring?

- Do you have plans to work your Siberian or compete in one of the canine sports?

The breeder is not being intrusive; he/she needs to understand the type of home you will be able to provide in order to make the right match.

Do not be offended by this. The breeder is doing it for both the dog's benefit and also for yours.

Steer clear of a breeder who does not ask you questions. He or she may be more interested in making money out of the puppies rather than ensuring that they go to good homes.

They may also have taken other short cuts, which may prove disastrous, and very expensive, in terms of vet bills or plain heartache.

The breeder needs to be confident that you can provide a suitable home for one of their precious puppies.

Puppy
watching

A litter of Siberian puppies is totally irresistible. Looking like cuddly teddies, they bear little resemblance to the wolf-like adults they will become. Every puppy seems to say: "Take me home" and it is hard to keep a cool head. However, you must try to put your feelings to one side so that you can make an informed choice.

You need to be 100 per cent confident that the breeding stock is healthy, and the puppies have been reared with love and care, before making a commitment to buy.

Viewing a litter

It is a good idea to have mental checklist of what to look out for when you visit a breeder. You want to see:

- A clean, hygienic environment.

- Puppies who are out-going, friendly, and eager to meet you.

- A sweet-natured mother who is ready to show off her puppies.

- Pups that are well covered, but not pot-bellied (which could be an indication of worms).

- Bright eyes, with no sign of soreness or discharge.

- Clean ears that smell fresh.

- No discharge from the eyes or nose.

- Clean rear ends – matting could indicate upset tummies.

- Lively pups that are keen to play.

It is important that you see the mother with her puppies as this will give you a good idea of the temperament they are likely to inherit. It is also helpful if you can see other close relatives so you can assess the type and temperament that the breeder produces.

In most cases, you will not be able to see the father (sire) as most breeders will travel some distance to find a stud dog that is not too close to their own bloodlines and complements their bitch. However, you should be able to see photos of him and find out how he is bred as well as being given details of his show/working record.

Health Issues

Like all purebred dogs, Siberian Huskies have a predisposition to some health disorders, which may or may not be inherited. Ask the breeder for a full history of the parents and preceding generations to see if there are any issues you need to be aware of.

For more information, see Breed Specific Conditions, page 182.

Companion puppy

If your Siberian's role in life is to be a companion dog, you should allow the breeder to guide your choice. It is tempting to go for the pup that comes up to you first, or the one that makes you laugh as he chases his siblings. But the breeder will have spent hours and hours watching the puppies as they have developed from newborns.

He/she therefore has an in-depth knowledge of how the puppies interact with each other, with other dogs in the family, how they relate to people, and how they cope with new experiences.

This is invaluable information when making the right

match; the breeder will also take into account your family set up and lifestyle and will help you to pick the most suitable puppy.

Show puppy

Do you have ambitions to exhibit your Siberian in the show ring? If this is the case you need to make your intentions clear to the breeder so you can select a puppy that has the potential to be successful in the ring. The aim is to find a Sibe who will, when full grown, meet the stipulations set down in the Breed Standard. This is no easy matter when a puppy is only eight weeks old, so it is worth recruiting an expert to evaluate the litter. The breeder will also help you make a choice as he/she will only want their best quality dogs to go on show.

Working dog

The Siberian Husky has a strong work ethic and with the appropriate training he will make his mark in many of the canine sports. If you plan to work your Siberian in a team, temperament, as well as having the correct conformation, is hugely important.

You want a high-drive dog who can withstand the rigours of working under harness. He needs to work in a team, and he needs to fulfil a particular role within the team. For example, a lead dog needs to be bold but he must also listen to the instructions of the dog driver, whereas a swing or point dog can follow the lead. A wheel dog, working at the back of the team, just in front of the rig, needs a certain type of confidence to cope with the proximity of a fast moving vehicle.

There are some Siberians who cannot take the pressure of working in a team, and if this is the case you need to accept the situation and find another outlet for your dog's energy and intelligence.

Watch the puppies' reactions to get an idea of the individual personalities.

A Siberian friendly home

It may seem an age before your puppy is ready to leave the breeder and move to his new home. But you can fill the time by getting your home ready, and buying the equipment you will need.

These preparations apply to a new puppy but, in reality, they are the means of creating an environment that is safe and secure for your Siberian Husky throughout his life.

In the home

Nothing is safe when a puppy is about – and this is certainly true of the adventurous Siberian. Everything is new and exciting for a young puppy; it all needs thorough investigation – and this usually means testing with mouth and teeth. One thing is certain – a free-ranging Siberian puppy cannot be trusted! Remember, it is not only your prized possessions that are under threat; equally relevant is the damage a puppy can inflict on himself.

Trailing electric cables are a major hazard so these will need to be secured out of reach. You will need to make sure all cupboards and storage units cannot be opened – or broken into.

This applies particularly in the kitchen where you may store cleaning materials, and other substances, which could be toxic to dogs. There are a number of household plants that are poisonous, so these will need to relocated, along with breakable ornaments.

It would be wise to declare upstairs off-limits as negotiating stairs can be hazardous in terms of potential accidents as well as putting unnecessary strain on a puppy's joints. The best way of doing this is to fix a baby gate at the bottom of the stairs.

In the garden

The Siberian Husky is known as the Houdini of the dog world – you have been warned! The Siberian is a great escape artist, so providing a safe, secure outside environment is of paramount importance. Fencing needs to be 2m (6ft) in height, and should be checked on a regular basis to ensure there are no gaps or places where a dog could dig his way out. If you have a gate leading out of the garden it should have a secure fastening, and you would be advised to put up a sign, reminding visitors to shut the gate.

Siberians are enthusiastic diggers, so you may decide to fence off part of the garden so the lawn – and your prized plants – are not ruined. Bear in mind, there are a number of plants that are toxic to dogs so you need to you need to check these out on the internet and remove them, or restrict access to them before your puppy comes home.

Swimming pools and ponds should be covered as most puppies are fearless and, although it is easy for a puppy to take the plunge, it is virtually impossible for him to get out unaided.

You will also need to designate a toileting area. This will assist the house-training process, and it will also make cleaning up easier. For information on house-training, see page 92.

House rules

Before your puppy comes home, hold a family conference to decide on the house rules. You need to decide which rooms your puppy will have access to, and establish whether he is to be allowed on the furniture or not. Given the eventual size of a Siberian, and his shedding coat, you may decide that sofas and armchairs are off-limits – but it is all a matter of working out what is right for you and your family.

The most important consideration is to be consistent so that your Sibe understands the rules. He will become very confused if one member of the sofa allows him on the sofa for a cuddle and then someone else tells him off when he tries to do the same thing. Your puppy needs to know where his boundaries lie otherwise he will push his luck and will not respect you as the decision-maker.

Buying equipment

There are some essential items of equipment you will need for your Siberian. If you choose wisely, much of it will last for many years to come.

Indoor crate

Rearing a puppy is so much easier if you invest in an indoor crate. It provides a safe haven for your puppy at night, when you have to go out during the day, and at other times when you cannot supervise him.

A puppy needs a base where he feels safe and secure, and where he can rest undisturbed.

Below: A Sibe puppy needs to understand what is – and what is not – allowed.

An indoor crate provides the perfect den, and many adults continue to use them throughout their lives. So you will need to make sure you buy a crate that will be big enough to accommodate your Sibe when he is fully grown. He needs to be able to stand up and turn around.

You will also need to consider where you are going to locate the crate. The kitchen is usually the most suitable place as this is the hub of family life. Find a snug corner where the puppy can rest when he wants to, but where he can also see what is going on around him, and still be with the family.

Playpen

This is not essential but playpens are becoming increasingly popular with puppy owners. You can set up the playpen, line it with bedding and equip it with toys so your puppy has a safe area to play in – and cannot get into mischief.

Beds and bedding

The crate and playpen will need to be lined with bedding. The best type to buy is synthetic fleece which is warm and cosy. It is also machine washable and easy to dry. An added advantage is that moisture soaks through the bedding, so when your puppy is going through the house training process there is no risk of him being left in a wet bed. If you have purchased a crate, you may not feel the need to buy an extra bed, but if your Sibe enjoys joining the family in the sitting room, for example, it will be useful if he has his own base.

There is an amazing array of dog-beds to chose from – duvets, bean bags, cushions, baskets, igloos, mini-four posters – so you can take your pick.

Bear in mind that the well-furred Siberian can overheat and so he will generally prefer a bed that is not too cushioned or too enclosed. It is also worth pointing out that some beds prove irresistible as far as chewing is concerned, so delay making a major investment until your Siberian has outgrown the destructive, puppy phase. There are some individuals who never lose the desire to chew, and if you have one of these, you should restrict your dog to a crate or a hard, plastic bed that can be lined with bedding.

Collar and lead

You may think that it is not worth buying a collar for the first few weeks, but the sooner your pup gets used to it, the better (see Wearing a collar, page 130). A nylon lightweight collar is recommended, as most puppies will accept it without making a fuss. Be careful when you are fitting the collar that is not too tight, but equally not too loose; a good guideline is to make sure you can fit two of your fingers under the collar.

The Siberian was born to pull and many owners find that a harness works better with this breed. Make sure the harness you buy is correctly fitted, which means you will probably get through a couple of harnesses while your puppy is growing.

There are plenty of different leads to choose from, but in the case of a Siberian, it must be super strong. A leather lead is the best option as it will withstand the strain and is kind to your hand. You also need to make sure it has a secure trigger fastening.

An extending lead can be a useful purchase as you can give your Siberian limited freedom when it is not safe or permitted to allow him off lead. However, you should never use it when walking alongside roads; if your Sibe pulls unexpectedly and the lead extends further than you intend, it could have disastrous consequences.

ID

Your Siberian needs to wear some form of ID when he is out in public places. This can be in the form of a disc, engraved with your contact details, attached to the collar. When your Siberian is full-grown, you can buy an embroidered collar with your contact details,

Time for some shopping therapy while you wait for your puppy to arrive in his new home...

which eliminates the danger of the disc becoming detached from the collar.

You may also wish to consider a permanent form of ID. Increasingly breeders are getting puppies micro-chipped before they go to their new homes. A micro-chip is the size of a grain of rice. It is 'injected' under the skin, usually between the shoulder blades, with a special needle. It has some tiny barbs on it, which dig into the tissue around where it lies, so it does not migrate from that spot.

Each chip has its own unique identification number that can only be read by a special scanner. That ID number is then registered on a national database with your name and details, so that if ever your dog is lost, he can be taken to any vet or rescue centre where he is scanned and then you are contacted.

If your puppy has not been micro-chipped, you can ask your vet to do it, maybe when he goes along for his vaccinations.

Bowls

Your Siberian will need two bowls; one for food, and one for fresh drinking water, which should always be readily available. A stainless steel bowl is a good choice for a food bowl.

Plastic bowls will almost certainly be chewed, and

there is a danger that bacteria can collect in the small cracks that may appear. You can opt for a second stainless steel bowl for drinking water, or you may prefer a heavier ceramic bowl, which will not be knocked over so easily.

Food

The breeder will let you know what your puppy is eating and should provide a full diet sheet to guide you through the first six months of your puppy's feeding regime – how much they are eating per meal, how many meals per day, when to increase the amounts given per meal and when to reduce the meals per day. The breeder may provide you with some food when you go and collect your puppy, but it is worth making enquiries in advance about the availability of the brand that is recommended.

Grooming gear

To get your puppy accustomed to grooming, start with a soft brush. As the adult coat comes through – and the shedding starts – you will need a curry comb and a rake which help you get rid of the dead hair.

In addition you will need:

- Nail-clippers: The guillotine type are easy to use.

- Toothbrush and toothpaste: Choose between a long-handled toothbrush or a finger brush, whichever you find easiest. There are flavoured canine toothpastes on the market, which your dog will enjoy.

- Cotton-wool or medicated ear wipes.

Toys

The Siberian has a high prey drive, and so anything that is soft and furry – and moves – is a sure fire winner! There are a number of chaser toys on the market, made of a variety of materials from faux fur to rabbit skin. Siberians also like to tug, so fleece or knotted rope tuggy toys will go down well. Both tug and chaser toys give you a means of interacting with your Siberian which helps to enrich your relationship.

All toys should be checked regularly for wear and tear, and do not leave your puppy with a toy when he is not being supervised. The exception to this is if you buy a hard, rubber kong, which can be stuffed with food. This is 100 per cent safe and will give your Siberian an occupation when he needs to be left home alone.

Finding a vet

Before your puppy arrives home, you should register

Facing page: A puppy needs to get used to being groomed from an early age.

with a vet. Visit some of the vets in your local area, and speak to other pet owners that you might know, to find out who they recommend. It is so important to find a good vet, almost as much as finding a good doctor for yourself. You need to find someone with whom you can build a good rapport and have complete faith in. Word of mouth is really the best recommendation.

When you contact a veterinary practice, find out the following:

- Does the surgery run an appointment system?

- What are the arrangements for emergency, out-of-hours cover?

- What facilities are available at the practice?

- Do the vets in the practice have experience in treating Siberian Huskies?

If you are satisfied with what you find, and the staff appear to be helpful and friendly, book an appointment so your puppy can have a health check a couple of days after you collect him.

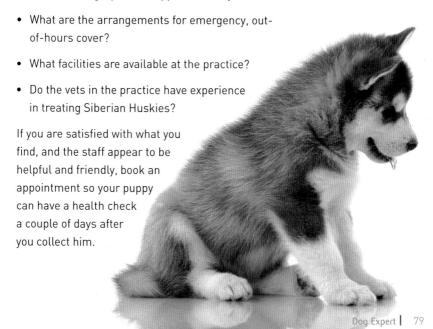

Settling in

When you first arrive home with your puppy, be careful not to overwhelm him. You and your family are hugely excited, but the puppy is in a completely strange environment with new sounds, smells and sights. This is a daunting experience, even for the boldest of pups.

Some puppies are very confident, wanting to play straightaway and quickly making friends; others need a little longer. Keep a close check on your Siberian's body language and reactions so you can proceed at a pace he is comfortable with.

First, let him explore the garden. He will probably need to relieve himself after the journey home, so take him to the allocated toileting area and, when he performs, give him plenty of praise.

When you take your puppy indoors, let him investigate again. Show him his crate, and encourage him to enter by throwing in a treat. Let him sniff,

and allow him to go in and out as he wants to. Later on, when he is tired, you can put him in the crate while you stay in the room. In this way he will learn to settle and will not think he is being abandoned.

It is a good idea to feed your puppy in his crate, at least to begin with, as this helps to build up a positive association. It will not be long before your Sibe sees his crate as his own special den and will go there as a matter of choice. Some owners place a blanket over the crate, covering the back and sides, so that it is even more cosy and den-like.

Meeting the family

Resist the temptation of inviting friends and neighbours to come and meet the new arrival; your puppy needs to focus on getting to know his new family for the first few days. Try not to swamp your Siberian with too much attention – he needs a chance to explore and find his feet. There will be plenty of time for cuddles later on!

If you have children in the family, you need to keep everything as calm as possible.

The Siberian will make an outstanding family companion but a sense of mutual respect needs to be established. Your small, cuddly puppy will soon grow into a energetic, athletic adult, with lots of ideas of his own, so both dog and children need to know where the boundaries lie.

Children must learn to:

- Allow the puppy to eat his food without interfering
- Leave him to rest undisturbed when he goes to his crate or his bed.
- Engage in games that involve dog toys – not children's toys
- Treat him with respect, never prodding, poking or teasing him.

A Siberian puppy must learn:

- That children should never be chased or nipped, and fingers must never be mouthed
- To keep four feet on the ground, never jumping up and knocking children off-balance.
- To keep his distance at family mealtimes, settling in his crate or in his bed.

Bear in mind, it is easy for a puppy with a strong prey instinct to become over-excited by children running around and behaving unpredictably, and this can easily lead to mouthing and nipping.

The best plan is to get the children to sit on the floor and give them all a treat. Each child can then call the puppy, stroke him, and offer a treat. In this way the puppy realises that it is not a free for all, and that he needs to interact with each child calmly and sensibly in order to get his treat.

If he tries to nip or mouth, make sure there is a toy at the ready, so his attention can be diverted to something he is allowed to bite. If you do this consistently, he will learn to inhibit his desire to mouth when he is interacting with people.

Right from the start, impose a rule that the children are not allowed to pick up or carry the puppy. They can cuddle him when they are sitting on the floor. This may sound a little severe, but a wriggly puppy can be dropped in an instant, sometimes with disastrous consequences.

Involve all family members with your puppy's day-to-day care; this will enable the bond to develop with the whole family as opposed to just one person. Encourage the children to train and reward the puppy, teaching him to follow their commands without question.

The animal family

Siberian Huskies are team players, and it feels more natural for them to live with other canines rather than being the family's sole dog. Siberians have an

Siberians enjoy each other's company.

affinity with each other but will also get on well with other breeds. Obviously, interactions need to be supervised in the early stages to get the relationship started on a good footing.

In an ideal scenario, introduce your resident dog to your new Sibe puppy at the breeder's home. This works well, as the puppy feels secure and the adult dog is not threatened. But if this is not possible, allow your dog to smell the puppy's bedding (the bedding supplied by the breeder is fine) before they actually meet so he familiarises himself with the puppy's scent.

The garden is the best place for introducing the puppy, as the adult will regard it as neutral territory. He will probably take a great interest in the puppy and sniff him all over.

Most puppies are naturally submissive in this situation, and your pup may lick the other dog's mouth or roll over on to his back. Try not to interfere as this is the natural way that dogs get to know each other.

You will only need to intervene if the older dog is too boisterous, and alarms the puppy. In this case, it is a good idea to put the adult on his lead so you have some measure of control.

It rarely takes long for an adult to accept a puppy, as he does not constitute a threat. This will be underlined if you make a big fuss of the older dog so that he has no reason to feel jealous.

Feline friends

Cats and Siberian Huskies are not a good mix as the Sibe's strong prey drive poses a real threat. If a Siberian puppy is brought up with a cat, his instinct to chase will be curbed – but he should never be trusted. No matter how well-behaved he as at home, he will always see the neighbourhood cats as fair game. He may live peaceably with the family cat for years and then suddenly, for no apparent reason, give chase – sometimes with tragic consequences.

If you are attempting to introduce your Siberian puppy to the resident cat, it may be easier to confine him in a carrier for the first couple of meetings so your puppy has a chance to make his acquaintance in a controlled situation. Keep calling your puppy to you and rewarding him so that he does not get obsessed with cat watching. You can then graduate to holding your puppy while the cat is free, again rewarding him with a treat every time he responds to you and looks away from the cat. When you allow your puppy to go free, make sure the cat has an easy escape route, just in case he tries to chase.

This is an on-going process but all the time your Siberian is learning that he is rewarded for ignoring the cat. In time, the pair will learn to co-exist but never leave them alone together when you are not there to supervise.

Feeding

The breeder will generally provide enough food for the first few days so the puppy does not have to cope with a change in diet – and possible digestive upset – along with all the stress of moving home.

Some puppies eat up their food from the first meal onwards, others are more concerned by their new surroundings and are too distracted to eat. Do not worry unduly if your puppy seems disinterested in his food for the first day or so. Give him 10 minutes to eat what he wants and then remove the leftovers and start afresh at the next meal.

Obviously if you have any concerns about your puppy in the first few days, seek advice from your vet.

If your Siberian seems to lose interest in his food, try feeding him in his crate where he can eat in peace and will not be so distracted.

It is also advisable to work at your Siberian's food manners so he never feels threatened when he is eating and does not become protective of his food

Facing page: Settling into a new home is an exhausting business...

bowl. You can do this by giving him half his ration, and then dropping food around his bowl.

This will stop him guarding his bowl and, at the same time, he will see your presence in a positive light. You can also call him away from the bowl and reward him with some food – maybe something extra special – which he can take from your hand.

Start doing this as soon as your puppy arrives in his new home, and continue working on it throughout his life.

The first night

Your puppy will have spent the first weeks of his life with his mother or curled up with his siblings. He is then taken from everything he knows as familiar, lavished with attention by his new family – and then comes bed time when he is left all alone. It is little wonder that he feels abandoned.

The best plan is to establish a night-time routine, and then stick to it so that your puppy knows what is expected of him.

Take your puppy into the garden to relieve himself, and then settle him in his crate. Some people leave a low light on for the puppy at night for the first week, others have tried a radio as company or a ticking clock.

A covered hot-water bottle, filled with warm water, can also be a comfort. Like people, puppies are all individuals and what works for one, does not necessarily work for another, so it is a matter of trial and error.

Be very positive when you leave your puppy on his own; do not linger, or keep returning; this will make the situation more difficult. It is inevitable that he will protest to begin with, but if you stick to your routine, he will accept that he gets left at night – but you always return in the morning.

Rescued dogs

Settling an older, rescued dog in the home is very similar to a puppy in as much as you will need to make the same preparations regarding his homecoming.

As with a puppy, an older dog will need you to be consistent, so start as you mean to go on.

There is often an initial honeymoon period when you bring a rescued dog home, where he will be on his best behaviour for the first few weeks.

It is after these first couple of weeks that the true nature of the dog will show, so be prepared for subtle changes in his behaviour.

It may be advisable to register with a reputable training club, so you can seek advice on any training or behavioural issues at an early stage.

Above all, remember that a rescued dog ceases to be a rescued dog the moment he enters his forever home and should therefore be treated like any other family pet.

House training

This is an aspect of training that first-time owners dread, but the Siberian is a clean and clever dog and if you start as you mean to go on, it will not be long before he understands what is required.

The key to successful house training is vigilance and consistency. If you establish a routine, and you stick to it, your puppy will understand what is required.

Equally, you must be there to supervise him at all times – except when he is safely tucked up in his crate. It is when a puppy is left to wander from room to room that accidents are most likely to happen.

As discussed earlier, you will have allocated a toileting area in your garden when preparing for your puppy's homecoming.

You need to take your puppy to this area every time

he needs to relieve himself so he builds up an association and knows why you have brought him out to the garden.

Establish a routine and make sure you take your puppy out at the following times:

- First thing in the morning
- After mealtimes
- On waking from a sleep
- Following a play session
- Last thing at night.

A puppy should be taken out to relieve himself every two hours as an absolute minimum. If you can manage an hourly trip out, so much the better.

The more often your puppy gets it 'right', the quicker he will learn to be clean in the house. It helps if you use a verbal cue, such as "busy", when your pup is performing and, in time, this will trigger the desired response.

Do not be tempted to put your puppy out on the doorstep in the hope that he will toilet on his own. Most pups simply sit there, waiting to get back inside the house!

No matter how bad the weather is, accompany your

puppy and give him lots of praise when he performs correctly. Do not rush back inside as soon as he has finished, your puppy might start to delay in the hope of prolonging his time outside with you.

Praise him, have a quick game – and then you can both return indoors.

When accidents happen

No matter how vigilant you are there are bound to be accidents. If you witness the accident, take your puppy outside immediately, and give him lots of praise if he finishes his business out there.

If you are not there when he has an accident, do not scold him when you discover what has happened. He will not remember what he has done and will not understand why you are cross with him.

Simply clean it up and resolve to be more vigilant next time.

Make sure you use a deodoriser, available in pet stores, when you clean up, otherwise your pup will be drawn to the smell and may be tempted to use the same spot again.

Choosing a diet

There are so many different types of dog food on sale – all claiming to be the best – so how do you know what is likely to suit your Siberian Husky? A well balanced diet is key to your Sibe's health and wellbeing, so you need to do your homework in order to make the right decision.

The Siberian Husky was bred to work for hours on end, in harsh conditions where food was scarce. As a result he has developed a specialised digestive system, which means he can make do on very little.

It is all about quality rather than quantity and so the ideal diet is high in fat and protein and low in cereal. The Siberian is a relatively big, active dog but he does not need the same amount of food as other breeds of similar size and stature.

If he is fed too much, he cannot digest the food and will suffer from diarrhoea. This can be remedied by reducing the quantity you feed, but bear in mind that diarrhoea can cause serious problems in young puppies as they dehydrate very rapidly. It is therefore better to keep a very close check on what you are feeding to prevent the problem arising,

When choosing a diet, there are basically three categories to choose from:

Complete

This is probably the most popular diet as it is easy to feed and is specially formulated with all the nutrients your dog needs. This means that you should not add any supplements or you may upset the nutritional balance.

Most complete diets come in different life stages: puppy, adult maintenance and senior, so this means that your Siberian is getting what he needs when he is growing, during adulthood, and as he becomes older. You can even get prescription diets for dogs with particular health issues.

With a Siberian Husky you need to select a top-quality diet that is high in fat and protein – but do not follow the manufacturer's feeding guide, your Sibe will need substantially less than is recommended.

Canned/pouches

This type of food, known as wet food, is usually fed with hard biscuit, and most Siberians find it very appetising. However, the ingredients – and the nutritional value – do vary significantly between the different brands so you will need to check the label. The more natural wet foods contain rice rather than other cereals containing gluten, so select this type to avoid allergic reactions.

Bear in mind that wet foods, as their name indicates, often have a high moisture content, so you need to be sure your Siberian is getting all the nutrition he needs.

Homemade

There are some owners who like to prepare meals especially for their dogs – and it is probably much appreciated. The danger is that although the food is tasty, and your Siberian may appreciate the variety, you cannot be sure that it has the correct nutritional balance.

If this is a route you want to go down, you will need to find out the exact ratio of fats, carbohydrates, proteins, minerals and vitamins that are needed, which is quite an undertaking.

The Barf (Biologically Appropriate Raw Food) diet is another, more natural approach to feeding. Dogs are fed a diet mimicking what they would have eaten in the wild, consisting of raw meat, bone, muscle, fat, and vegetable matter. This diet works very well for the Siberian Husky; if you are worried about handling raw meat there are now a number of companies that specialise in producing the Barf diet in frozen form.

Feeding regime

When your puppy arrives in his new home he will need four meals, evenly spaced throughout the day. You may decide to keep to the diet recommended by your puppy's breeder, and if your pup is thriving there is no need to change. However, if your puppy is not doing well on the food, or you have problems with supply, you will need to make a change.

When switching diets, it is very important to do it on a gradual basis, changing over from one food to the next, a little at a time, and spreading the transition over a week to 10 days. This will avoid the risk of digestive upset.

When your puppy is around 12 weeks, you can cut out one of his meals; he may well have started to leave some of his food indicating he is ready to do this. By six months, he can move on to two meals a day – a regime that will suit him for the rest of his life.

Faddy feeders

If your Siberian is reluctant to eat, especially during
the settling in period, it is hard not to try to tempt his
appetite. One look from those dark eyes is enough to
melt your heart, stirring you to greater efforts to find
a food that he will really like. At first you may add
some gravy, then you may try some chicken... The
clever Sibe will quickly realise that if he holds out,
tastier treats will follow. This is a bad game to play
as not only will you run out of tempting
delicacies, you will also be losing your
Siberian's respect.

If your dog is turning up his nose at
mealtimes, give him 10 minutes to eat what
he wants, and then take up his bowl and give
him fresh food at his next mealtime. Do not
feed him treats in between meals. If you
continue this regime for a couple of days,
your Siberian will realise that there is no
percentage in holding out for better food
as it never materialises.

In most cases, this is just a 'trying
it on' phase, and if you cope with
common sense, you will soon
return to the status quo and your
Siberian will be content with his

*Below: Your puppy will
need four meals until
he is around three
months of age.*

normal rations. If, however, your dog refuses all food for more than 24 hours you need to observe his behaviour to see if there are any signs of ill health, which may involve the need for a veterinary check up.

Bones and chews

Puppies love to chew, and many adults also enjoy gnawing on a bone. A raw marrow bone is ideal, but make sure it is always given under supervision.

Rawhide chews are best avoided; it is all too easy for a dog to bite off a chunk and swallow it, with the danger of it then causing a blockage. The Siberian can become possessive when he has a bone so work on his food manners, so that he learns not to guard when he has food. You also need to train him to "leave" his bone when you give him a verbal cue (see page 145) so that he is ready to give it up on request.

Ideal weight

In order to help to keep your Siberian fit and healthy it is necessary to monitor his weight. Obesity is a major problem among the canine population, and a dog that is fed too much, often coupled with insufficient exercise, is likely to pile on the pounds.

A dog that is carrying too much weight is vulnerable to many health issues; he has a poorer quality of life as he cannot exercise properly, and he will almost certainly have a reduced life expectancy.

The Siberian has a big coat, but it lies close to the contours of his body, making it fairly easy to assess his condition. When looking at your dog from above, you should be able to see a definite 'waist'. You should be able to feel his ribs, but not see them. To keep a check on your Siberian's weight, get into the habit of visiting your veterinary surgery on a monthly basis so that you can weigh him. You can keep a record and make adjustments to his diet if necessary.

If you are concerned that your Siberian is putting on too much weight, or equally if you think he is underweight, consult your vet, who will help you to plan a suitable diet.

Below: When your puppy is teething he will have an irresistible desire to chew.

Caring for your Siberian Husky

The Siberian is a tough, no-nonsense breed, but he has been transplanted from his life as a working sled dog in the far North and so we need to ensure that we cater for his particular needs.

Coat care

The Siberian's double coat, with its soft, dense undercoat and the outer coat consisting of straight hair that lies close to the body, is a feature of the breed.

It has incredible insulating qualities which were invaluable in the Arctic home of his forebears but rather less so in the temperate climates of Europe and many parts of the USA where he is kept in growing numbers.

The Siberian's shedding coat is legendary; this phenomenon happens twice yearly, and for a few weeks your house will be awash with hair.

Daily grooming is essential to loosen and remove dead hair. This will make your Sibe feel more comfortable and will help, in some measure, to contain the spread of dog hair... In between moults, the coat needs regular brushing to keep it in good order.

The Siberian does not particularly like being groomed so you need to start work at an early age to accustom him to being handled.

Initially, he will wriggle and attempt to mouth you, but just ignore his protests.

Hold him steady for a few moments, and reward him

when he is still. A puppy needs to learn that it is OK to be touched all over; if you fail to do this, he may try to warn you off by growling, which could develop into more problematic behaviour.

Start by handling your puppy all over, stroking him from his head to his tail. Lift up each paw in turn, and reward him with a treat when he co-operates.

Then roll him over on to his back and tickle his tummy; this is a very vulnerable position for a dog to adopt, so do not force the issue. Be firm but gentle, and give your Sibe lots of praise when he does as you ask.

When you start grooming, place your puppy on a rubber mat to prevent him from slipping.

The puppy's coat changes as he matures. To begin with it will be soft and fluffy, then it changes in texture, becoming coarser and denser. Initially, all you need to do is work through the coat with a soft brush.

As the adult coat comes through you will need a brush with stiffer bristles.

During coat shedding, a curry comb is useful for loosening the undercoat, and a rake can be used for the feathering on the back legs and the guard hairs of the topcoat.

Routine care

In addition to grooming, you will need to carry out some routine care.

Eyes

Check the eyes for signs of soreness or discharge.

If there is debris around the eye, you can use a piece of cotton-wool (a separate piece for each eye) for cleaning. However, if there is discharge from the eye, you should book a visit to the vet who can examine the eyes and prescribe the appropriate treatment.

Ears

You will need to check the ears to ensure they are clean and free from odour.

If the ear is dirty, you can clean it using medicated ear-wipes or damp cotton-wool. Be careful not to probe into the ear canal or you could do more harm than good. If your dog's ears appear to be particularly dirty and foul-smelling, consult your vet who will prescribe the appropriate treatment.

Teeth

Dental disease is increasing among dogs so teeth cleaning should be seen as an essential part of your care regime. Bear in mind, the build up of tartar on

Ears need to be checked and cleaned when necessary.

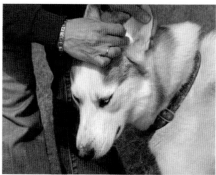

Regular brushing prevents tooth decay and gum disease.

Trim nails little but often.

the teeth can result in tooth decay, gum infection and bad breath, and if it is allowed to accumulate, you may have no option but to get the teeth cleaned under anaesthetic.

When your Siberian is still a puppy, accustom him to teeth cleaning so it becomes a matter of routine. Dog toothpaste comes in a variety of meaty flavours which your Sibe will like, so you can start by putting toothpaste on your finger and gently rubbing his teeth.

You can then progress to using a finger brush or a toothbrush, whichever you find most convenient.

Remember to reward your Siberian when he co-operates and then he will positively look forward to his teeth-cleaning sessions.

Nails

Nail trimming is a task dreaded by many owners – and many dogs – but, again, if you start early on, your Siberian will get used to the task you have to perform and will not fight against it. A Siberian can have white or dark-coloured nails, depending in his coat colour.

If your Sibe has white nails, your job is easier as you will be able to see the quick – the vein that runs through the nail – and avoid it.

In dark-coloured nails, the quick is obscured and if it is nicked it will bleed profusely. This will be uncomfortable for your Siberian, and he will remember it next time you attempt to trim his nails.

The best policy is to trim little and often so the nails don't grow too long, and you do not risk cutting too much and catching the quick.

The Siberian Husky also has dewclaws, located just above the foot which act rather like our thumbs. These also need to be trimmed otherwise they will grow into your Siberian's leg.

If you are worried about trimming nails, go to your vet so you can see it done properly. If you are still concerned, you can always use the services of a professional groomer.

Exercise

This is a breed that needs extensive exercise – but do not get carried away! If you allow a puppy unlimited exercise, he will be putting too much strain on his vulnerable, growing joints, which could result in permanent damage.

To begin with, your puppy will get as much exercise as he needs playing in the garden.

Once he has completed his vaccinations, you can

take him out on the lead so that he will become acquainted with the outside world.

Free running exercise – which can only be allowed in enclosed areas – can be increased very gradually as your Siberian grows. Once your Siberian is mature, he will relish as much exercise as you can give him.

Hopefully you have taken on a Siberian because you also want to take lots of exercise, and so you can start teaching him to run with you while he is on a long lead.

Ideally, you will also be planning to exercise his mind and body by working him or getting involved in one of the canine sports (see page 152).

Playing games

This is a great way of providing physical exercise and mental stimulation which is very useful for the Siberian as you can tire him out within the confines of your garden!

The Siberian likes to use his brain and he will be keen to interact with you and earn rewards.

The more you play with him, the more he will enjoy it and the two of you can become increasingly inventive with games of search and retrieve, and maybe some trick training thrown in for good measure.

Facing page: A Siberian Husky can only be allowed to free run in a safe, enclosed area.

If your Sibe is a bit of a foodie, there is a game you can play which will use his mental energies and make use of his sense of smell.

Once in a while, do not give your Siberian his food in a bowl but scatter it over a small area in the garden.

Let your Sibe see what you are doing, and then encourage him to "find" his dinner. There are few dogs who can resist this, and they will become fully focused on the task of seeking out their food.

The older Siberian

We are fortunate that Siberian Huskies enjoy a good life expectancy. Most will make double figures, and it is not unknown for dogs to reach their early to mid teens.

However, it is inevitable that your Siberian will slow up as he gets older so you need to keep a close check to monitor this change.

The older Siberian may sleep more and he may be reluctant to go for longer walks. He may show signs of stiffness when he gets up from his bed, but these generally ease when he starts moving.

Some older Siberians may have impaired vision, and some may become a little deaf, but as long as their senses do not deteriorate dramatically, this is something older dogs learn to live with.

If you treat your older dog with kindness and consideration, he will enjoy his later years and suffer the minimum of discomfort. He may be slowing up but he can still enjoy a good quality of life.

It is advisable to switch him over to a senior diet, which is more suited to his needs, and you may need to adjust the quantity, as he will not be burning up the calories as he did when he was younger and more energetic.

Make sure his sleeping quarters are warm and free from draughts, and if he gets wet, make sure you dry him thoroughly.

Most important of all, be guided by your Siberian. He will have good days when he feels up to going for a walk, and other days when he would prefer to potter in the garden.

If you have a younger dog at home, this may stimulate your Sibe to take more of an interest in what is going on, but make sure he is not pestered as he needs to rest undisturbed when he is tired.

Letting go

Inevitably there comes a time when your Siberian Husky is not enjoying a good quality of life, and you need to make the painful decision to let him go.

We would all wish that our dogs died, painlessly, in their sleep but, unfortunately, this is rarely the case.

However, we can allow our dogs to die with dignity, and to suffer as a little as possible, and this should be our way of saying thank you for the wonderful companionship they have given us.

When you feel the time is drawing close, talk to your vet who will be able to make an objective assessment of your Siberian's condition and will help you to make the right decision.

This is the hardest thing you will ever have to do as a dog owner, and it is only natural to grieve for your beloved Sibe.

But eventually, you will be able to look back on the happy memories of times spent together, and this will bring much comfort.

You may, in time, feel that your life is not complete without a Siberian, and you will feel ready to welcome a new puppy into your home.

Facing page: You need to monitor your dog's quality of life as he grows older.

Social skills

To live in the modern world, without fear and anxieties, a Siberian Husky needs to receive an education in social skills so that he learns to cope calmly and confidently in a wide variety of situations.

Early learning

The breeder will have begun a programme of socialisation by getting the puppies used to all the sights and sounds of a busy household.

You need to continue this when your pup arrives in his new home, making sure he is not worried by household equipment, such as the vacuum cleaner or the washing machine, and that he gets used to unexpected noises from the radio and television.

To begin with, your puppy needs to get used to all the members of his new family (see Meeting the Family, page 82), but then you should give him the opportunity to meet other people who come to the house. If you do not have children of your own,

make sure your puppy has the chance to meet and play with other people's children – making sure interactions are always supervised – so he learns that humans come in small sizes, too.

Home alone

The Siberian is a loyal and affectionate dog and within weeks of arriving in his new home, he will form a strong bond with his human pack. This is brilliant, but be careful. A Siberian also needs to learn to cope on his own, otherwise he will develop separation anxiety.

This happens when a dog panics if he is left on his own or becomes so bored that he seeks to find his own entertainment. Instead of settling quietly until his family return, the anxious dog will become increasingly distressed, and the bored dog will become increasingly frustrated.

In both cases, behaviour will deteriorate with the dog resorting to whining or continual barking or howling; he may become destructive, and he may even soil his sleeping quarters.

This should never be seen as a compliment – a sign of how much your Siberian Husky loves you or needs you to provide mental stimulation. It is simply a lack of training, which causes your dog acute distress because he cannot relax and settle. Right from the start, you need to accustom your dog to short periods on his own. Ideally, settle him in his crate with a boredom busting toy, such as a kong, filled with food, and leave him alone for a short period. When you return, do not make a big fuss of him. You could even wait a few minutes before you go to his crate, just to let him know that you are back, but it's no big deal.

Gradually increase the amount of time you leave your Siberian so that you are confident that he will settle happily for a couple of hours. Keep leaving rituals to a minimum so he does not start getting worried as he anticipates your departure, and do not make a big fuss of him when you return. In this way your Siberian will learn that arrivals and departures are part of daily life and he will be able to cope when he is home alone.

The outside world

When your puppy has completed his vaccinations, he is ready to venture into the outside world. As a breed, the Siberian Husky is generally confident and self-assured but there is a lot for a youngster to take on board, so do not swamp him with too many new experiences when you first set out.

Obviously you need to work at lead-training (see

page 132) before you set out on your first expedition. There will be plenty of distractions to cope with, so you do not want additional problems of coping with a dog that is pulling on the lead.

So, hopefully, you can set off with your Siberian walking by your side on a loose lead. He may need additional encouragement when you venture further afield – or he may try to pull your shoulder out of joint – so arm yourself with some extra special treats, which will give him a good reason to focus on you when required!

Start socialising your puppy in a quiet area with light traffic, and only progress to a busier place when he is ready. There is so much to see and hear – people (maybe carrying bags or umbrellas), pushchairs, bicycles, cars, lorries, machinery – so give your puppy a chance to take it all in.

If he does appear worried, do not fall into the trap of sympathising with him or he will think that there really is something to fear. The best plan is to give him a little space so he does not have to confront whatever he is frightened of, and distract him with a few treats.

Then ask him to walk past the scary thing, giving it a wide berth and rewarding him for any forward movement. As his confidence increases, you can get

a little closer but do not be impatient. It is better to
make a little progress and build on it the following day.

Dog to dog meetings

Your pup also needs to continue his education in
canine manners, started by his mother and by his
littermates, as he needs to be able to greet all dogs
calmly, giving the signals that say he is friendly. The
Siberian Husky is not an aggressive dog and so you
are unlikely to have problems. However, he will have
to encounter dogs when he is on the lead, which can
put him at a disadvantage.

*Below: A puppy starts
his social education
when he is with his
mother and littermates.*

To counteract this, you will need to organise some meetings and greetings so your Siberian can build up the social skills he requires. Find a friend who has a dog with a bombproof temperament and visit their house. Allow the two dogs to play in the garden for 10 minutes or so. Do not prolong the game as you do not want your youngster to become over-excited, or overwhelmed.

Once the two dogs have had a few play dates at home, go for a walk in a safe, enclosed area and allow them to exercise together off lead. They will interact with each other, but their focus will shift periodically as they will be distracted by other sights and smells.

Extend your Siberian's circle of acquaintance by finding other friends who have dogs of sound temperament, ideally ranging over a number of different breeds. The more your Sibe practices meeting and greeting, the better he will become at reading body language and assessing other dogs' intentions.

Training classes

A training class will give your Siberian the opportunity to work alongside other dogs in a controlled situation, and he will also learn to focus on you in a different, distracting environment. Both these lessons will be vital as your dog matures. However, the training class needs to be of the highest calibre or you risk doing more harm than good.

Before you go along with your puppy, attend a class as an observer to make sure you are happy with what goes on.

Find out the following:

- How much training experience do the instructors have?

- Are the classes divided into appropriate age categories?

- Do they use positive, reward-based training methods?

- Do any of the instructors have experience with Siberian Huskies?

If the training class is well run, it is certainly worth attending.

Both you and your Sibe will learn useful training exercises. It will increase his social skills, and you will have the chance to talk to lots of like-minded dog enthusiasts.

Training guidelines

There is no doubting a Siberian Husky's intelligence – some would say he is too clever for his own good! He has an independent mind and likes to take the initiative but, on the plus side, he is prepared to listen as long as he has an owner he respects...

You will be keen to get started, but in your rush to get training underway, do not neglect the fundamentals that could make the difference between success and failure.

You need to get into the mindset of a Siberian, working out what makes him tick and, equally, what makes him switch off.

Decide on your priorities for training, set realistic targets, and then think of ways of making your training both positive and rewarding.

When you start training, try to observe the following guidelines:

Choose an area that is free from distractions so your puppy will focus on you. You can move on to a more challenging environment as your pup progresses.

Do not train your puppy just after he has eaten or when you have returned from exercise. He will either be too full, or too tired, to concentrate.

Do not train if you are in a bad mood, or if you are short of time – these sessions always end in disaster!

Providing a worthwhile reward is an essential tool in training. You will probably get the best results if you use some extra special food treats, such as cheese or cooked liver.

Some Siberians get very focused on a favourite toy – but the urge to destroy it can get in the way of training!

If you decide to use a toy, make sure it is only brought out for training sessions so that it accrues added value. Keep your verbal cues simple, and always use the same one for each exercise. For example, when you ask your puppy to go into the Down position, the cue is "Down", not "Lie Down", Get Down", or anything else.

Remember your Sibe does not speak English; he associates the sound of the word with the action. If your dog is finding an exercise difficult, break it down into small steps so it is easier to understand.

Do not make your training sessions boring and repetitious. If training is dull, your Sibe will lose focus and go off to find something more interesting to do!

Do not train for too long, particularly with a young puppy that has a very short attention span, and always end training sessions on a positive note.

This does not necessarily mean getting an exercise right. If your pup is tired and making mistakes, ask him to do a simple exercise so you have the opportunity to praise and reward him.

You may well find that he benefits from having a break and will make better progress next time you try.

Remember that if your Siberian is rewarded for a behaviour, he is likely to repeat it – so make sure you are 100 per cent consistent and always reward the 'right' behaviour.

First lessons

Like all puppies, a young Siberian Husky will soak up new experiences like a sponge, so training should start from the time your pup arrives in his new home.

Wearing a collar

You may, or may not, want your Siberian to wear a collar all the time – you may be planning to use a harness when you take him out – but he will need to have some form of ID and this will generally be a disc attached to a collar or an embroidered collar with contact details.

Therefore, he will need to get used to the feel of a collar so that he learns to ignore it. The best plan is to accustom your pup to wearing a soft collar for a few minutes at a time until he gets used to it.

Fit the collar so that you can get at least two fingers between the collar and his neck. Then have a game to distract his attention.

This will work for a few moments; then he will stop,

put his back leg up behind his head and scratch away at the peculiar itchy thing round his neck, which feels so odd.

Bend down, rotate the collar, pat him on the head and distract him by playing with a toy or giving him a treat. Once he has worn the collar for a few minutes each day, he will soon ignore it and become used to it.

Remember, never leave the collar on the puppy unsupervised, especially when he is outside in the garden, or when he is in his crate, as it is could get snagged, causing serious injury.

Walking on the lead

This is a simple exercise – but for a Siberian who was bred to pull it can be a real problem. Pulling sleds was the name of the game for a working dog, but the Sibe has effortlessly transferred this 'talent' to lead waking. His instinct is to pull and so you need to work hard to prevent this behaviour becoming ingrained.

You may decide to use a harness in the long run but it is advisable to start off with collar and lead to teach what is required:

Once your puppy is used to the collar, take him outside into your secure garden where there are no distractions.

Attach the lead and, to begin with, allow him to wander with the lead trailing, making sure it does not become snagged. Then pick up the lead and follow the pup where he wants to go; he needs to get used to the sensation of being attached to you.

The next stage is to get your Siberian to follow you, and for this you will need some treats. To give yourself the best chance of success, make sure the treats are high value – cheese, sausage or cooked liver – so your Sibe is motivated to work with you.

Show him you have a treat in your hand, and then encourage him to follow you. Walk a few paces, and if he is walking with you, stop and reward him. If he puts on the brakes, simply change direction and lure him with the treat.

Next introduce some changes of direction so your puppy is walking confidently alongside you. At this stage, introduce a verbal cue "Heel" when your puppy is in the correct position.

You can then graduate to walking your puppy outside the home – as long as he has completed his vaccination programme – starting in quiet areas and building up to busier environments.

Come when called

For most Siberian Huskies, the opportunities for free running exercise are limited – but a reliable recall is still important. You would be foolish to trust your Siberian to come back when he is in hot pursuit of a rabbit – but there are many other times when you need to recall him, such as when he is outside playing in the garden or when you have the chance to exercise him in a safe, enclosed area.

The key to successful recall training is to start early, and to teach your Sibe to focus on you, regardless of distractions:

Hopefully, the breeder will have laid the foundations simply by calling the puppies to "Come" when it is dinnertime, or when they are moving from one place to another.

You can build on this when your puppy arrives in his new home, calling him to "Come" when he is in a confined space, such as the kitchen.

This is a good place to build up a positive association with the verbal cue – particularly if you ask your puppy to "Come" to get his food!

The next stage is to transfer the lesson to the garden. Arm yourself with some treats, and wait until your puppy is distracted. Then call him, using a higher-pitched, excited tone of voice.

At this stage, a puppy wants to be with you, so capitalise on this, keep practising the verbal cue, and reward your puppy with a treat and lots of praise when he comes to you.

Now you are ready to introduce some distractions. Try calling him when someone else is in the garden, or wait a few minutes until he is investigating a really interesting scent.

When he responds, make a really big fuss of him and give him some extra treats so he knows it is worth his while to come to you. If your puppy responds, immediately reward him with a treat.

If he is slow to come, run away a few steps and then call again, making yourself sound really exciting. Jump up and down, open your arms wide to welcome him; it doesn't matter how silly you look, he needs to see you as the most fun person in the world.

When you have a reliable recall in the garden, you can try it outside the home, providing you have a safe, enclosed area you can use for free running exercise.

Make sure you have top-quality treats; ask your Siberian to "Sit" and reward him before letting him off the lead. In this way, he knows you have something really tasty on offer, which means he has an added incentive to respond to the recall.

Do not make the mistake of only asking your dog to come at the end of his allotted exercise period.

What is the point in coming back to you if all you do is clip on his lead, marking the end of his free time?

Instead, call your dog at random times, giving him a treat and a stroke, and then letting him go free again. In this way, coming to you – and focusing on you – is always rewarding.

Stationary exercises

The Sit and Down are easy to teach, and mastering these exercises will be rewarding for both you and your Siberian Husky. They are useful in a wide variety of situations and ensure that you always have a measure of control.

Sit

The best method is to lure your Siberian into position, and for this you can use a treat or his food bowl.

Hold the reward (a treat or food bowl) above his head. As he looks up, he will lower his hindquarters and go into a sit.

Practise this a few times and when your puppy understands what you are asking, introduce the

verbal cue, "Sit". When your Sibe understands the exercise, he will respond to the verbal cue alone, and you will not need to reward him every time he sits. However, it is a good idea to give him a treat on a random basis when he co-operates to keep him guessing!

Down

This is an important lesson, and can be a lifesaver if an emergency arises and you need to bring your Siberian to an instant halt.

You can start with your dog in a Sit or a Stand for this exercise. Stand or kneel in front of him and show him you have a treat in your hand. Hold the treat just in front of his nose and slowly lower it towards the ground, between his front legs.

As your Sibe follows the treat he will go down on his front legs and, in a few moments, his hindquarters will follow.

Close your hand over the treat so he doesn't cheat and get the treat before he is in the correct position. As soon as he is in the Down, give him the treat and lots of praise.

Keep practising, and when your Sibe understands what you want, introduce the verbal cue "Down".

Below: Youngsters find it hard to concentrate, so build up the duration of the Down exercise in easy stages.

Control exercises

These are important to master, as they are useful in a variety of situations and will hopefully result in a Siberian Husky who will think before he acts.

Wait

This exercise teaches your Siberian Husky to "Wait" in position until you give the next command. It differs from the Stay exercise, where he must stay where you have left him for a more prolonged period.

The most useful application of "Wait" is when you are getting your dog out of the car and you need him to stay in position until you clip on his lead.

Start with your puppy on the lead to give you a greater chance of success. Ask him to "Sit", then stand in front him. Step back one pace, holding your hand, palm flat, facing him.

Wait a second and then come back to stand in front of him. You can then reward him and release him with a word, such as "OK". Practise this a few times, waiting a little longer before you reward him, and then introduce the verbal cue "Wait".

You can reinforce the lesson by using it in different situations, such as asking your Sibe to "Wait" before you put his food bowl down.

Stay

You need to differentiate this exercise from the Wait by using a different hand signal and a different verbal cue. Start with your Sibe in the Down, as he most likely to be secure in this position. Stand by his side and then step forwards, with your hand held back, palm facing the dog. Step back, release him, and then reward him.

Practise until your Sibe understands the exercise and then introduce the verbal cue "Stay". Gradually increase the distance you can leave your puppy, and increase the challenge by walking around him – and even stepping over him – so that he learns he must "Stay" until you release him.

Leave

A response to this verbal cue means that your Siberian Husky will learn to give up a toy on request, and it follows that he will give up anything when he is asked, which is very useful if he has got hold of a forbidden object.

This not simply a matter of obeying the verbal cue to "Leave"; it is establishing the status quo where you are the decision-maker and your Siberian is ready to co-operate with you.

This is particularly important with a Siberian Husky who can become possessive with favourite toys or places of high value, such as the sofa, or even your bed!

The "Leave" command can be taught quite easily when you are first playing with your puppy. As you gently, take a toy from his mouth, introduce the verbal cue, "Leave", and then praise him. If he is reluctant, swap the toy for another toy or a treat. This will usually do the trick.

Do not try to pull the toy from his mouth if he refuses to give it up, as you will make the situation confrontational.

Let the toy go 'dead' in your hand, and then swap it for a new toy, or a really high-value treat so this becomes the better option.

Remember to make a big fuss of your Sibe when he does as you ask so that he learns that co-operation is always the best – and most rewarding – option. This exercise can also be used if your Siberian takes up a favourite position, such as on the sofa, and refuses to budge.

Again the strategy is not to be confrontational but to offer him a better reward, such as a treat or a toy, and then call him to you.

As far as your Siberian is concerned, he has not been forced to give up the thing he values, he has simply been offered something better – a win, win situation.

Opportunities for Siberian Huskies

The Siberian Husky was bred to work, using his speed, strength and considerable intelligence. This is a dog that must use his brain, but you need to find a sport or activity that suits his temperament.

Good Citizen Scheme

The Kennel Club Good Citizen Scheme was introduced to promote responsible dog ownership, and to teach dogs basic good manners. In the US there is one test; in the UK there are four award levels: Puppy Foundation, Bronze, Silver and Gold. Taking part in this scheme is an excellent way of socialising your Siberian Husky with other dogs as well as teaching him to be obedient. Exercises within the scheme include:

- Walking on lead
- Road walking
- Control at door/gate.
- Food manners
- Recall
- Stay
- Send to bed

- Emergency stop.

- Agility

In Agility, the dog completes an obstacle course under the guidance of his owner. You need a good element of control, as the dog works off the lead. In competition, each dog completes the course individually and is assessed on both time and accuracy. The dog that completes the course with the fewest faults, in the fastest time, wins the class. The obstacles include an A-frame, a dog-walk, weaving poles, a seesaw, tunnels, and jumps. This is a great sport for Siberian Huskies as it gives the opportunity for both physical and mental exercise in a controlled environment. A good agility dog has to respond to his handler and use his own initiative, which fits in well with the Siberian temperament.

Competitive obedience

This is a sport where dog and handler are assessed together, completing a series of exercises including heelwork, recalls, retrieves, stays, sendaways and scent discrimination. The intelligent Sibe is more than capable of performing these exercises but he is not a dog to be drilled and will quickly switch off if training becomes dull and repetitious. To achieve top honours in this discipline requires intensive training as precision and accuracy are of

paramount importance – this may not always suit
the independent-minded Siberian Husky.

Rally O

If you do not want to get involved in the rigours of
Competitive Obedience, you may find that a sport
called Rally O is more to your liking. This is loosely
based on Obedience, and also has a few exercises
borrowed from Agility when you get to the highest
levels. Handler and dog must complete a course, in
the designated order, which has a variety of different
exercises that could number from 12 to 20. The
course is timed and the team must complete within
the time limit that is set, but there are no bonus
marks for speed. The great advantage of Rally O
is that it is very relaxed, and anyone can compete.
Indeed, it has proved very popular for handlers with
disabilities as they are able to work their dogs to a
high standard and compete on equal terms.

Canicross

This is the perfect sport for the Siberian Husky as it
involves long-distance, cross country running while
attached to his owner. This sport is a fun activity for
you and your dog, and if you become addicted you
can get involved in competitions.

The dog is fitted with a well-padded harness, and he

*Facing page: Canicross
– running with your Sibe
– is a excellent way of
providing exercise.*

is attached to his human partner via a bungee line that fastens on to a waist belt.

The dog needs to learn verbal cues to stop, start, go right or left, and to check his pace. If you want to keep fit and exercise your dog this is the sport for you.

Mushing

This is a sport which reflects the original work of sled dog teams and it has been adapted for temperate climates that do not have much snow. Competitors must drive a team of dogs pulling a sled (over snow) or a wheeled rig (on dry land) following a marked course; the winner is the first across the line.

There is a huge amount of work involved in training a team and building up fitness for long distance races, so you need to be dedicated. You also need enough room to accommodate a team of huskies at home...

Scootering/bikejoring

If you cannot keep a team of Siberians, why not try this sport where you only need one dog? With training, your Siberian will learn to run ahead while you follow behind on a bicycle or a scooter.

This is both fast and furious, and a fair amount of

skill is required to keep the correct tension on the long line so it does not become tangled in the front wheel. Safety is therefore of paramount importance.

Showing

The Siberian is more at home pulling a sled than exhibiting in a show ring but, nonetheless, he is a stunning sight when shown in peak condition.

This discipline is not just about looking good; a Siberian needs to learn how to behave in the ring so he can show himself off to advantage.

The best plan is to join ringcraft classes so you and your dog can practise working together amid distractions, find out about show ring etiquette – and discover all the tricks of the trade.

Your top priority is to give your Siberian a chance to use his brain.

Health care

The Siberian Husky is a tough dog bred to withstand the harshest of conditions. But like all breeds, he needs a comprehensive programme of preventative care and good management to keep him in the best of health.

Vaccinations

Dogs are subject to a number of contagious diseases. In the old days, these were killers, and resulted in heartbreak for many owners. Vaccinations have been developed, and the occurrence of the major infectious diseases is now very rare. However, this will only remain the case if all pet owners follow a strict policy of vaccinating their dogs.

There are vaccinations available for the following diseases:

Adenovirus: (Canine Adenovirus): This affects the liver; affected dogs have a classic 'blue eye'.

Distemper: A viral disease which causes chest and gastro-intestinal damage. The brain may also be affected, leading to fits and paralysis.

Parvovirus: Causes severe gastro enteritis, and most commonly affects puppies.

Leptospirosis: This bacterial disease is carried by rats and affects many mammals, including humans. It causes liver and kidney damage.

Rabies: A virus that affects the nervous system and is invariably fatal. The first signs are abnormal behavior, when the infected dog may bite another animal or a person. Paralysis and death follow.

Vaccination is compulsory in most countries. In the UK, dogs travelling overseas must be vaccinated.

Kennel cough: There are several strains of kennel cough, but they all result in a harsh, dry, cough. This disease is rarely fatal; in fact most dogs make a good recovery within a matter of weeks and show few signs of ill health while they are affected. However, kennel cough is highly infectious among dogs that live together so, for this reason, most boarding kennels will insist that your dog is protected by the vaccine, which is given as nose drops.

Lyme disease: This is a bacterial disease transmitted by ticks (see page 166). The first signs are limping, but the heart, kidneys and nervous system can also be affected. The ticks that transmit the disease occur in specific regions, such as the north-east states of the USA, some of the southern states, California and the upper Mississippi region. Lyme disease is still relatively rare in the UK so vaccinations are not routinely offered.

Vaccination programme

In the USA, the American Animal Hospital Association advises vaccination for core diseases, which they list as: distemper, adenovirus, parvovirus and rabies. The requirement for vaccinating for non-core diseases – leptospirosis, lyme disease and kennel cough – should be assessed depending on a dog's individual risk and his likely exposure to the disease.

In the UK, vaccinations are routinely given for distemper, adenovirus, leptospirosis and parvovirus.

In most cases, a puppy will start his vaccinations at around eight weeks of age, with the second part given a fortnight later. However, this does vary depending on the individual policy of veterinary practices, and the incidence of disease in your area. You should also talk to your vet about whether to give annual booster vaccinations.

Parasites

No matter how well you look after your Siberian Husky you will have to accept that parasites – internal and external – are ever present, and you need to take preventative action.

Internal parasites: As the name suggests, these parasites live inside your dog. Most will find a home in the digestive tract, but there is also a parasite that lives in the heart. If infestation is unchecked, a dog's health will be severely jeopardised, but routine preventative treatment is simple and effective.

External parasites: These parasites live on your dog's body – in his skin and fur, and sometimes in his ears.

Roundworm

This is found in the small intestine, and signs of infestation will be a poor coat, a pot belly, diarrhoea and lethargy. Pregnant mothers should be treated, but it is almost inevitable that parasites will be passed on to the puppies. For this reason, a breeder will start a worming programme, which you will need to continue. Ask your vet for advice on treatment, which will need to continue throughout your dog's life.

Tapeworm

Infection occurs when fleas and lice are ingested; the adult worm takes up residence in the small intestine, releasing mobile segments (which contain eggs) which can be seen in a dog's faeces as small rice-like grains.

The only other obvious sign of infestation is irritation of the anus. Again, routine preventative treatment is required throughout your Siberian's life.

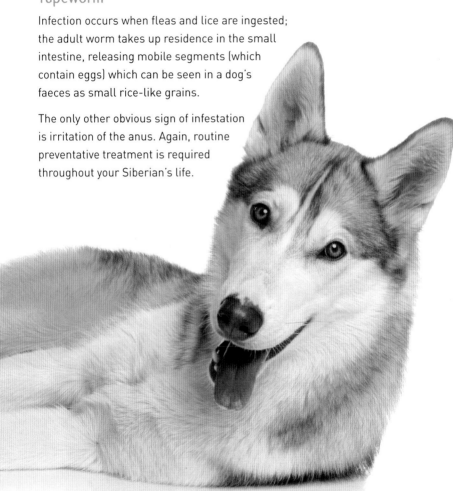

Heartworm

This parasite is transmitted by mosquitoes, and so will only occur where these insects thrive. A warm environment is needed for the parasite to develop, so it is more likely to be present in areas with a warm, humid climate.

However, it is found in all parts of the USA, although its prevalence does vary. At present, heartworm is rarely seen in the UK.

Heartworm live in the right side of the heart. Larvae can grow up to 14 inches (35cm) in length. A dog with heartworm is at severe risk from heart failure, so preventative treatment, as advised by your vet, is essential.

Dogs living in the USA should have regular blood tests to check for the presence of infection.

Lungworm

Lungworm, or *Angiostrongylus vasorum*, is a parasite that lives in the heart and major blood vessels supplying the lungs.

It can cause many problems, such as breathing difficulties, blood-clotting problems, sickness and diarrhoea, seizures, and can even be fatal.

The parasite is carried by slugs and snails, and the

dog becomes infected when ingesting these, often accidentally when rummaging through undergrowth. Lungworm is not common, but it is on the increase and a responsible owner should be aware of it.

Fortunately, it is easily preventable and even affected dogs usually make a full recovery if treated early enough. Your vet will be able to advise you on the risks in your area and what form of treatment may be required.

Fleas

A dog may carry dog fleas, cat fleas, and even human fleas. The flea stays on the dog only long enough to have a blood meal and to breed, but its presence will result in itching and scratching.

If your dog has an allergy to fleas – which is usually a reaction to the flea's saliva – he will scratch himself until he is raw.

Preventative treatment needs be administered on a routine basis; this can be in the form of a tablet, spot-on treatment, an insecticidal spray or shampoo. Ask your vet for advice on what product to use.

Bear in mind that the whole environment your dog lives in will need to be sprayed, and all other pets living in your home will also need to be treated.

How to detect fleas

You may suspect your dog has fleas, but how can you be sure? There are two methods to try.

Run a fine comb through your dog's coat, and see if you can detect the presence of fleas on the skin, or clinging to the comb. Alternatively, sit your dog on white paper and rub his back. This will dislodge faeces from the fleas, which will be visible as small brown specks. To double check, shake the specks on to damp cotton-wool (cotton). Flea faeces consists of the dried blood taken from the host, so if the specks turn a lighter shade of red, you know your dog has fleas.

Ticks

These are blood-sucking parasites, most frequently found in rural areas where sheep or deer are present. The main danger is their ability to pass lyme disease to both dogs and humans. Lyme disease is prevalent in some areas of the USA (see page 158), although it is still rare in the UK.

The treatment you give your dog for fleas generally works for ticks, but you should discuss the best product to use with your vet.

How to remove a tick

If you spot a tick on your dog, do not try to pluck it off as you risk leaving the hard mouth parts embedded in his skin. The best way to remove a tick is to use a fine pair of tweezers, or you can buy a tick remover. Grasp the tick head firmly and then pull the tick straight out from the skin. If you are using a tick remover, check the instructions, as some recommend a circular twist when pulling. When you have removed the tick, clean the area with mild soap and water.

Ear mites

These parasites live in the outer ear canal. The signs of infestation are a brown, waxy discharge, and your dog will continually shake his head and scratch his ear.

If you suspect your Siberian has ear mites, a visit to the vet will be needed so that medicated ear drops can be prescribed.

Fur mites

These small, white parasites are visible to the naked eye and are often referred to as 'walking dandruff'. They cause a scurfy coat and mild itchiness.

However, they are zoonetic – transferable to humans – so prompt treatment with an insecticide prescribed by your vet is essential.

Harvest mites

These are picked up from the undergrowth, and can be seen as a bright orange patch on the webbing between the toes, although this can be found elsewhere on the body, such as on the ear flaps.

Treatment is effective with the appropriate insecticide.

Skin mites

There are two types of parasite that burrow into a dog's skin. *Demodex canis* is transferred from a mother to her pups while they are feeding. Treatment is with a topical preparation, and sometimes antibiotics are needed.

The other skin mite is *Sarcoptes scabiei*, which causes intense itching and hair loss. It is highly contagious, so all dogs in a household will need to be treated, which involves repeated bathing with a medicated shampoo.

Common
ailments

As with all living animals, dogs can
be affected by a variety of ailments.
Most can be treated effectively after
consulting with your vet, who will
prescribe appropriate medication and
will advise you on how to care for your
dog's needs

Here are some of the more common problems that could affect your Siberian Husky with advice on how to deal with them.

Anal glands

These are two small sacs on either side of the anus, which produce a dark-brown secretion that dogs use when they mark their territory.

The anal glands should empty every time a dog defecates but if they become blocked or impacted, a dog will experience increasing discomfort. He may nibble at his rear end, or 'scoot' his bottom along the ground to relieve the irritation.

Treatment involves a trip to the vet, who will empty the glands manually. It is important to do this without delay or infection may occur.

Dental problems

Regular brushing prevents the accumulation of tartar which causes gum infection and tooth decay.

If it accumulates to the extent that you cannot remove it by brushing, the vet will need to intervene. In a situation such as this, an anaesthetic will need to be administered so the tartar can be removed manually.

Diarrhoea

There are many reasons why a dog has diarrhoea, but most commonly it is the result of scavenging, a sudden change of diet, or an adverse reaction to a particular type of food. In the case of the Siberian Husky, over-feeding can lead to digestive upset.

If your dog is suffering from diarrhoea, the first step is to withdraw food for a day. It is important that he does not dehydrate, so make sure that fresh drinking water is available.

However, drinking too much can increase the diarrhoea, which may be accompanied with vomiting, so limit how much he drinks at any one time.

After allowing the stomach to rest, feed a bland diet, such as white fish or chicken, with boiled rice, for a few days.

In most cases, your dog's motions will return to normal and you can resume normal feeding, although this should be done gradually.

However, if this fails to work and the diarrhoea persists for more than a few days, you should consult you vet. Your dog may have an infection, which needs to be treated with antibiotics, or the diarrhoea may indicate some other problem which needs expert diagnosis.

Ear infections

The Siberian Husky has erect ears. This means that air can circulate freely which minimises the risk of ear infections. However, it is important to check ears on a regular basis.

A healthy ear is clean with no sign of redness or inflammation, and no evidence of a waxy brown discharge or a foul odour.

If you see your dog scratching his ear, shaking his

head, or holding one ear at an odd angle, you will need to consult your vet.

The most likely causes are ear mites, an infection, or there may a foreign body, such as a grass seed, trapped in the ear.

Depending on the cause, treatment is with medicated ear drops, possibly containing antibiotics. If a foreign body is suspected, the vet will need to carry our further investigations.

Eye problems

The Siberian has medium-sized, almond-shaped eyes which should not protrude. This is important as a breed such as the Pug that has prominent eyes will be more vulnerable to injury.

Healthy eyes are bright and sparkling with no sign of discharge.

If your Siberian's eyes look red and sore, he is likely to be suffering from conjunctivitis. This may, or may not be accompanied with a watery or a crusty discharge.

Conjunctivitis can be caused by irritation to the eyeball, a bacterial or viral infection, it could be the result of an injury, or it could be an adverse reaction to pollen.

You will need to consult your vet for a correct diagnosis, but in the case of an infection, treatment with medicated eye drops is effective.

Conjunctivitis may also be the first sign of more serious inherited eye problems (see Entropion page 184, Pannus, page 186).

Foreign bodies

In the home, puppies – and some older dogs – cannot resist chewing anything that looks interesting. The Siberian is prone to destructive behaviour if he is bored and, with his strong teeth and powerful jaws, he can get through most materials.

The toys you choose for your dog should be suitably robust to withstand damage, but children's toys can be irresistible.

Some dogs will chew – and swallow – anything from socks, tights, and any other items from the laundry basket to golf balls and stones from the garden.

Obviously, these items are indigestible and could cause an obstruction in your dog's intestine, which is potentially lethal. The signs to look for are vomiting, and a tucked up posture. The dog will often be restless and will look as though he is in pain.

In this situation, you must get your dog to the vet

without delay, as surgery will be needed to remove the obstruction.

If you exercise your Siberian in long grass, you need to give him a thorough check when you return home. It is all too easy for grass seeds to find their way into orifices such as a nostril, down an ear or into the soft skin between the toes. This can result in an abscess and veterinary intervention will be required.

Heatstroke

Many owners fail to appreciate that a dog may suffer from over-heating on warm days, and not just on days when the temperature soars.

This is particularly the case with a Siberian Husky whose coat is designed for sub-zero temperatures.

However, do not make the mistake of clipping or shaving your dog's coat during the summer months; the undercoat is dual purpose, keeping him warm in the winter and cool in the summer.

Common sense should dictate how to manage your Siberian when the weather is hot. Avoid rigorous exercise in the middle of the day and make sure your dog has access to shady areas.

Be extra careful if you leave your Siberian in the car, as the temperature can rise dramatically – even on a cloudy day. Heatstroke can happen very rapidly, and unless you are able lower your dog's temperature, it can be fatal.

If your Siberian appears to be suffering from heatstroke, lie him flat and work at lowering his temperature by spraying him with cool water and covering him with wet towels.

As soon as he has made some recovery, take him to the vet where cold intravenous fluids can be administered.

Lameness/limping

There are a wide variety of reasons why a dog can go lame, from a simple muscle strain, to a fracture, ligament damage, or more complex problems with the joints, which may be inherited (see page 188).

If you are concerned about your dog, do not delay in seeking expert advice from your vet.

As your Siberian becomes more elderly, he may suffer from arthritis, which you will see as general stiffness, particularly when he gets up after resting.

It will help if you ensure his bed is in a warm draught-free location, and if your Siberian gets wet after exercise, you must dry him thoroughly.

If your Siberian seems to be in pain, consult your vet who will be able to help with pain relief medication.

Skin problems

The Siberian Husky can be prone to skin problems, and some may have an hereditary cause (see page 189). Fleas, and other external parasites can result in itching, and the skin can become very sore and inflamed if the dog has an allergic reaction.

Preventative treatment is obviously essential, but if you suspect an allergic reaction, you may need to seek veterinary advice.

Food intolerance and environmental factors, such as dust mites or pollen, can also cause major skin problems.

It is difficult to find the root cause, which can only be done by a process of elimination – that is, removing specific foods from the diet.

Breed
specific
conditions

Like all pedigree dogs, the Siberian
Husky does have a few breed-related
disorders. If diagnosed with any of the
diseases listed below, it is important to
remember that they can affect offspring
so breeding from affected dogs should
be discouraged.

There are now recognised screening tests to enable breeders to check for affected individuals and hence reduce the prevalence of these diseases within the breed.

DNA testing is also becoming more widely available, and as research into the different genetic diseases progresses, more DNA tests are being developed.

Eye disorders

The Siberian Husky is predisposed to a number of eye disorders and all dogs should undergo testing at 12 months of age.

This is important for pet dogs but it is an essential requirement for potential breeding stock.

Eye conditions include:

Canine Uveodermatological Syndrome

This is an autoimmune condition which causes loss of pigment in the skin and inflammation of the iris which can lead to blindness.

Entropion

This involves an in-rolling of the eyelids – usually the lower eyelid – which can result in damage to the retina. The condition may be minor or it may require surgery to correct it.

Generalised Progressive Retinal Atrophy (GPRA)

This is a condition which involves the destruction of the photoreceptors in the retina. As the disease progresses the retina shrivels up, resulting in total loss of vision. It is inherited as a X-linked factor in the Siberian Husky so males are more likely to be affected than females.

Glaucoma

The pressure of the fluid within the eyeball rises, causing considerable pain and eventual blindness if untreated.

Cataract

This is thought to be hereditary and involves the formation of a cataract/s at the back of the lens, usually evident at around six months of age. Screening is available for this condition.

Pannus

This is a long-term inflammation of the cornea, often accompanied by conjunctivitis. The degree of the problem varies but it can result in blindness. Treatment involves limiting the effects of the inflammation and minimising exposure to the ultra violet effects of the sun.

Persistent Pupillary Membrane

In the womb, the eye is covered with a membrane which supplies blood to it. If this fails to break down four to five weeks after birth, vision is affected to varying degrees.

Hypothyroidism

Sled dogs often have lower levels of thyroid than other breeds, but there is also a predisposition to an under-active thyroid gland.

This gland produces a hormone called thyroxine and low levels in the body produce symptoms which include: lethargy, cold intolerance, lack of appetite or constant hunger.

Other breed suffering from this condition become obese and have a thinning coat, but this is not the case with Siberians so it is important to be aware of the other signs to aid diagnosis. Treatment is with hormone replacement therapy.

Joint Problems

Degenerative Myelopathy

This affects the hind limbs and first becomes evident in middle age with a slow, progressive weakness, loss of co-ordination and muscle wastage.

The dog eventually loses the ability to walk, although he can still control both bladder and bowels. There is no effective treatment to date.

Hip dysplasia

This is a malformation of the hip joint where the head of the femur does not align with the cup of the hip socket. Resulting lameness ranges from mild to severe. Surgery can be effective. All potential breeding stock should be x-rayed and hip-scored.

Skin Conditions

Follicular dysplasia

Several puppies may be affected by this condition which is first seen at three to four months of age. The primary hairs of the body coat fall out and are not replaced; there is also a reddening of the undercoat.

Discoid Lupus Erythematosus

This results in loss of pigment of the nose, which may become grey and ulcerated. The lips, ears and external genitalia may also be affected. It is exacerbated by sunlight and so the most effective treatment is to apply sunblocks and minimise exposure to the sun.

Zinc-responsive dermatosis

A fairly common condition in Siberian Huskies, this is seen as a scabby, itchy skin which, if left untreated, results in baldness. It is unique to Northern sled breeds, and is caused by an inability to digest zinc unless high levels of vitamin A are present in the diet. A zinc supplement, prescribed by a vet, is usually effective.

Summing up

It may give the pet owner cause for concern to find out about health problems that may affect their dog. But it is important to bear in mind that acquiring some basic knowledge is an asset, as it will allow you to spot signs of trouble at an early stage.

Early diagnosis is very often the means to the most effective treatment. Fortunately, the Siberian Husky is a generally healthy and disease-free dog with his only visits to the vet being annual check-ups. In most cases, owners can look forward to enjoying many happy years with this outstanding companion.

Useful addresses

Breed & Kennel Clubs

Please contact your Kennel Club to obtain contact information about breed clubs in your area.

UK

The Kennel Club (UK)
1 Clarges Street London, W1J 8AB
Telephone: 0870 606 6750
Fax: 0207 518 1058
Web: www.thekennelclub.org.uk

USA

American Kennel Club (AKC)
5580 Centerview Drive, Raleigh, NC 27606.
Telephone: 919 233 9767
Fax: 919 233 3627
Email: info@akc.org
Web: www.akc.org

United Kennel Club (UKC)
100 E Kilgore Rd, Kalamazoo,
MI 49002-5584, USA.
Tel: 269 343 9020
Fax: 269 343 7037
Web:www.ukcdogs.com

Australia

Australian National Kennel Council (ANKC)
The Australian National Kennel Council is the administrative body for pure breed canine affairs in Australia. It does not, however, deal directly with dog exhibitors, breeders or judges. For information pertaining to breeders, clubs or shows, please contact the relevant State or Territory Body.

International

Fédération Cynologique Internationalé (FCI)
Place Albert 1er, 13, B-6530 Thuin, Belgium.
Tel: +32 71 59.12.38
Fax: +32 71 59.22.29
Web: www.fci.be

Training and behavior

UK

Association of Pet Dog Trainers
Telephone: 01285 810811
Web: www.apdt.co.uk

Canine Behaviour
Association of Pet Behaviour Counsellors
Telephone: 01386 751151
Web: www.apbc.org.uk

USA

Association of Pet Dog Trainers
Tel: 1 800 738 3647
Web: www.apdt.com

American College of Veterinary Behaviorists
Web: dacvb.org

American Veterinary Society of Animal Behavior
Web: www.avsabonline.org

Australia

APDT Australia Inc
Web: www.apdt.com.au

For details of regional behaviorists, contact the relevant State or Territory Controlling Body.

Activities
UK
Agility Club
www.agilityclub.co.uk

British Flyball Association
Telephone: 01628 829623
Web: www.flyball.org.uk

USA
North American Dog Agility Council
Web: www.nadac.com/

North American Flyball Association, Inc.
Tel/Fax: 800 318 6312
Web: www.flyball.org

Australia
Agility Dog Association of Australia
Tel: 0423 138 914
Web: www.adaa.com.au

NADAC Australia
Web: www.nadacaustralia.com

Australian Flyball Association
Tel: 0407 337 939
Web: www.flyball.org.au

International
World Canine Freestyle Organisation
Tel: (718) 332-8336
Web: www.worldcaninefreestyle.org

Health
UK
British Small Animal Veterinary Association
Tel: 01452 726700
Web: www.bsava.com

Royal College of Veterinary Surgeons
Tel: 0207 222 2001
Web: www.rcvs.org.uk

Alternative Veterinary Medicine Centre
Tel: 01367 710324
Web: www.alternativevet.org

USA
American Veterinary Medical Association
Tel: 800 248 2862
Web: www.avma.org

American College of Veterinary Surgeons
Tel: 301 916 0200
Toll Free: 877 217 2287
Web: www.acvs.org

Canine Eye Registration Foundation
The Veterinary Medical DataBases
1717 Philo Rd, PO Box 3007,
Urbana, IL 61803-3007
Tel: 217-693-4800
Fax: 217-693-4801
Web: www.vmdb.org/cerf.html

Orthopaedic Foundation of Animals
2300 E Nifong Boulevard
Columbia, Missouri, 65201-3806
Tel: 573 442-0418
Fax: 573 875-5073
Web: www.offa.org

American Holistic Veterinary Medical
Association
Tel: 410 569 0795
Web: www.ahvma.org

Australia
Australian Small Animal Veterinary
Association
Tel: 02 9431 5090
Web: www.asava.com.au

Australian Veterinary Association
Tel: 02 9431 5000
Web: www.ava.com.au

Australian College Veterinary Scientists
Tel: 07 3423 2016
Web: acvsc.org.au

Australian Holistic Vets
Web: www.ahv.com.au